I WAS TOLD THERE'D BE CAKE

I WAS TOLD THERE'D BE CAKE

essays

SLOANE CROSLEY

Published by Portobello Books Ltd 2008

Portobello Books Ltd
Twelve Addison Avenue
Holland Park
London
W11 4QR

First published in the United States of America by Riverhead Books, New York,
an imprint of the Penguin Group (USA) Inc in 2008

A CIP catalogue record is available from the British Library

9 8 7 6 5 4 3 2 1

ISBN 978 1 84627 185 1

www.portobellobooks.com

Text designed by Tiffany Estreicher

Printed in Great Britain by CPI Bookmarque, Croydon

From and for Nettie

AUTHOR'S NOTE

I have changed the names of some individuals, and in some instances also modified or changed their identifying features, to preserve their anonymity. Except in the case of my family. Their names are their names just as my name is my name just as your name is your name. That is until someone comes along and changes it for a book of essays. In that instance, your name is my name. But not literally.

Also, in a couple of cases, composite characters have been created or timelines have been compressed. The goal was to maintain people's privacy without damaging the integrity of the essays. The other goal was to capture people using the brush strokes I felt defined them best. Perhaps they would have chosen different strokes. They are, after all, what it takes to rule the world.

CONTENTS

THE PONY PROBLEM

As most New Yorkers have done, I have given serious and generous thought to the state of my apartment should I get killed during the day. Say someone pushes me onto the subway tracks. Or I get accidentally blown up. Or a woman with a headset and a baby carriage wheels over my big toe, backing me into some scaffolding, which shakes loose a lead pipe, which lands on my skull. What then? After the ambulance, the hospital, the funeral, the trays of cheese cubes on foil toothpicks . . .

Back in the apartment I never should have left, the bed has gone unmade and the dishes unwashed. The day I get shot in a bodega (buying cigarettes, naturally) will in all likelihood be the day before laundry Sunday and the day after I decided to clean out my closet, got bored halfway through, and opted to watch sitcoms in my prom dress instead. I have pictured my loved ones coming to my apartment to collect my things and I have hoped that it would only be "lived-in" messy—bras drying on the shower curtain rod, muddy sneakers by the door. But that is never going to happen. My dust balls alone have a manifest destiny that drives them far beyond the ruffle of the same name.

I like to think that these hypothetical loved ones would persist in their devotion to dead me no matter what. They would literally be blinded by grief, too upset putting sweaters in boxes to notice that I hadn't dry-cleaned them in a year. That is, until one of them made his or her way to the kitchen.

"Where are you going?" my father would ask.

"Packing up her bedroom's much too painful," my mother would tell him, choking back the tears. "I'm going to start on the kitchen."

This is the part I dread. This is the part where my mother would open the drawer beneath my sink only to discover my stash of plastic toy ponies. There are about seven of them in there. Correction: one's a Pegasus, blue with ice skates. The rest vary in size, texture, and realism. Some are covered in brown felt, some have rhinestone eyes. Some come with their own grooming brushes; others with the price sticker still on their haunches. If they arrived in plastic and cardboard packaging, they remain unopened as if they will appreciate like Star Wars figurines. Perhaps they are not the dirtiest of dirty secrets, but they're about as high as one can get on the oddity scale without a ringer like toenail clippings.

I'm not exactly sure how the ponies happened. Though I have an inkling: "Can I get you anything?" I'll say, getting up from a dinner table, "Coffee, tea, a pony?" People rarely laugh at this, especially if they've heard it before. "This party's supposed to be fun," a friend will say. "Really?" I'll respond, "Will there be pony rides?" It's a nervous tic and a cheap joke, cheapened further by the frequency with which I use it. For that same reason, it's hard to weed out of my speech—most of the time I don't even realize I'm saying it. There are little elements in a person's life, minor fibers that become unintentionally tangled with our personality. Sometimes it's a patent phrase, sometimes it's a perfume, sometimes it's a wristwatch. For me, it is the constant referencing of ponies.

I don't even like ponies. If I made one of my throwaway equine requests and someone produced an actual pony, Juan Valdez–style, I would run very fast in the other direction. During a few summers at camp, I rode a chronically dehydrated pony named Brandy who would jolt down without notice to lick the grass outside the corral and I would careen forward, my helmet tipping to cover my eyes. I do, however, like ponies in the abstract. Who doesn't? It's like those movies with animated insects. Sure, the baby cockroach seems cute with CGI eyelashes, but how would you feel about fifty of her real-life counterparts living in your oven? And that's precisely the manner in which the ponies clomped their way into my regular speech: abstractly. "I have something for you," a guy will say on our first date. "Is it a pony?" No. It's usually a movie ticket or his cell phone number or a slobbery tongue kiss. But on our second date, if I ask again, I'm pretty sure I'm getting a pony.

And thus the pony drawer came to be. It's uncomfortable to admit, but almost every guy I have ever dated has unwittingly made a contribution to the stable. The retro pony from the '50s was from the most thoughtful guy I have ever known. The one with the glitter horseshoes was from a boy who would later turn out to be gay. The one with the rainbow haunches was from a pot dealer, and the one with the price tag stuck on the back was given to me by a narcissist who was so impressed with his gift he forgot to remove the sticker. Each one of them marks the beginning of a relationship. I don't mean to hint. It's *not* a hint, it's a flat-out demand: I. Want. A. Pony. I think what happens is that young relationships are eager to build up a romantic repertoire of private jokes, especially in the city where there's not always a great "how we met" story behind every great love affair. People meet at bars, through mutual friends, on dating sites, or because they work in the same industry. Just once a guy asked me out between two express stops on the N train. We were holding the same pole and he said, "I know this sounds crazy but would you like to go to a very public place and have a drink with me?" I looked into his seemingly non-psycho-killing, rent-paying, Sunday *Times*–subscribing eyes and said, "Yes. Yes, I would." He never bought me a pony. But he didn't have to.

If I subtract the overarching strangeness of being a grown woman with a toy collection, I like to think of the ponies as a tribute to my type—I date people for whom it would occur to them to do this. This is not such a bad thing. These are men who are creative and kind. They hold open doors and pour wine. If I joined a cult, I like to think they would come rescue me. No, the fulfilling of the request isn't the problem. It's the requesting that's off. They don't know yet that I make it all the time and I don't have the heart to tell them how whorish I am with my asking. For them, it's a deleted scene out of *Good Will Hunting*. For me, it's *Groundhog Day*. They have no reason to believe they're being unoriginal. Probably because they're not: I am. What am I asking when I ask for a pony but to be taken for more unique than I probably am?

The ponies, if by accident, have come to represent the most overtly sentimental part of my life. Because all of these relationships have ended, they have ended more or less badly. No affair that begins with such an orchestrated overture can end on a simple note. What I am left with is the relics of those relationships.

After a breakup, I'll conduct the normal breakup rituals. I'll cut up photographs, erase voice mails, gather his dark concert T-shirts I once slept in and douse them with bleach before I use them to clean my bathtub. But not the ponies. When I go to throw them away, I feel like a mother about to slap her child for the first time, to cross a line she never intended to cross. She's spitting mad. The arm flies up. And it never comes down.

Yet I feel a pressure to do something with the ponies. Statistically speaking, my chances of getting smacked on the head with a lead pipe are increasing every time I lock the door behind me. Also, a drawer full of beady-eyed toys is insanely creepy. But what to do?

Actual love letters I do in stages. I biannually clean out drawers of nonsensical items—receipts, loose double-A batteries, rubber bands of indeterminate origin—and stumble across a love letter. Unable to throw it out, I stick it in another drawer, crammed at the bottom, until I clean that one out, too, and finally throw the letter out. One romantic note generally goes through a minimum of three locales before it gets tossed out for good. But the ponies are uncrammable. They're three-dimensional and bubblegum-scented and impossible to hide, even from myself. Every time I open the drawer, it's a trip down Memory Lane, which, if you don't turn off at the right exit, merges straight into the Masochistic Nostalgia Highway. They are too embarrassing to leave out in the open, facing west like a collection of china elephants. They are too many to slide under the sofa. They are too plastic to wedge behind the radiator. I want to send them around the world like the Travelocity gnome, have them come back to me years from now when I have an attic in which to shut them away. As if all this weren't enough, there is that flash of my mother dressed in black, staring aghast into the open kitchen drawer. In a city that provides so many strange options to be immortalized by the local tabloids, it is just as important to avoid humiliation in death as it is in life.

"What is it?" my father would shout, imagining all the things you never like to think of your father imagining: flavored condoms, pregnancy tests, a complete set of Third Reich collectors' cards.

"Look!" my mother would howl, picking up Ranch Princess Pony (with matching bridle and real horseshoe charm necklace!) by her faux flaxen mane. Just before she passed out.

My first thought is to go to the Salvation Army and donate the ponies to the children. But the notion turns me into an insta-hippie—the ponies have bad karma. I wouldn't just be giving some kid Stargazer (with the glow-in-the-dark mane), I would be giving her Manic-Depressive Simon, who talked back

6

to billboards and infomercials and kicked me in his sleep. My next idea is to leave the ponies in the trash for a homeless person to find and sell on the street. But I can't risk seeing them on a table with used books and polyester scarves as I walk to the subway each morning. I think about burying them in the park but have my doubts about the ponies' biodegradability. I think about burning them, melting them into a puddle of plastic as their real-life counterparts were once melted for glue. Maybe I'll just sneak out to the reservoir after dark with a raft made from pool noodles and rubber bands and give them a Viking funeral.

While each subsequent idea is tilled from a progressively more unsophisticated plot, I know that I can't simply throw the ponies out with the recyling. The ponies have their roots in me, not the other person. They are *my* nervous habit, *my* odd little secret. While each serves as a memory of a specific individual, each memory is filtered through the same brain: mine. The ponies are a part of me—they deserve better than that. The keeping of love letters suddenly seems like a petty crime. I have the romantic equivalent of a body in the freezer.

So I put the ponies in a black plastic bag, grabbing them out of their drawer like a jewel thief who, for the sake of urgency, does not consider the preciousness of each object. I tie the bag in a knot, leave the apartment, and take them with me on the subway. I get on a sparsely populated car, drop them between my legs, and begin casually pushing them further under the seat with my heels. Then, just as casually, I forget to take them with me when I get up. I leave them there on the N train, bound for Brooklyn.

Of course, the second the doors shut, I realize what I have done. Actually, that's not true. The second the doors shut, I feel great. Sneaky and great and nostalgia-free.

The second after that I realize what I have done. In my effort to liberate myself from the ponies, I have given some poor girl at the end of the subway car a solid reason to think she might not make it back to her apartment that night: a suspiciously abandoned unmarked package on public transport. I wonder what must be racing through her mind as she sits motionless, unable to turn her gaze away from the lumpy plastic bag. I wonder if she flashes back to her apartment—to the dust, to the expired yogurt in the fridge, to the terrible DVDs that she won't be able to explain were "a gift." Perhaps she has her own holy grail of humiliation. Perhaps there's a collection of porcelain bunnies in the medicine cabinet.

In any case, the ponies are gone. They are on their way to a borough where eventually they will hit the end of the line and cycle back into the heart of the city. Unless the bomb squad finds them first. They are finally out of my sight and not even an 8.5 on the Nostalgia Richter Scale can summon them back. I created them and now I have uncreated them and there is nothing I can do about it. Except maybe continue to look both ways before crossing the street and avoid areas with a high saturation of random violence. I breathe a sigh of resolute relief. From now on I will make a conscious effort to remember—should I find myself face-to-face or pipe-to-skull with the end of my life—that the real proof that I have tried to love and that people have tried to love me back was never going to fit in a kitchen drawer.

CHRISTMAS IN JULY

I have never met two people more afraid of their house burning down than my parents. Their Westchester insurance policy contains the same level of fire and earthquake protection as their Californian home-owning counterparts. Their sets of fireplace pokers are manifold, each distancing the poker (my dad) from the pokee (the fire) farther than the last. For major holiday dinners, there is no such thing as a "fire in the background." The flaming abscess in the living room wall is always in the foreground, dominating the attention and the conversation.

"It's a good fire, Denis," says my mother, standing yards away from it.

My father contemplates this, having conducted a staring match with the fire for almost an hour. It's hard to say who's winning.

"I don't like the look of that piece there." He points. "It's smoking."

"It's *fine*." This from my sister, who twice has left the house without setting the alarm and once broke a mercury thermometer on the garage floor. Her credibility is shot.

He gets up to grab a poker. My mother takes a step forward.

"Holy . . . Denis, be careful!"

I make a move to assist my father, though I know he won't let me. He makes a kind of sped-up tsk-tsk-tsk-tsk noise and puts his hand up. Please note my parents are not afraid of burning their house down. *They are afraid of their house burning down.* To them, the threat is always an outside force—a neighbor's errant flame-thrower, a burglar who smokes, or, in all likelihood, a youngest child.

My father "fixes" the fire and draws the metal mesh curtain shut, followed by the glass doors. It looks exactly the same as it did before. We continue to stare at it as if waiting for it to speak. We don't have much time. Distant relatives will be arriving shortly and we'll have to act normal.

On birthdays, "Blow the candles out!" was not a euphemism for "Make a wish!" It was said in the same tone puberty-pumped boys use to tell their mothers to get out of their rooms at inopportune moments. A "blow the fucking candles out," if you will. And I did. Once I came home from a birthday party down the block, regaling my parents with tapered tales of sparklers and trendy birthday accoutrements called "trick candles." I figured if sparklers were good enough for the Horowitzes, if singing candles didn't engulf *their* kitchen cabinets with life-destroying flames . . .

"This is me hinting," I clarified.

"At what?" said my mother. "That you want to be a pyromaniac when you grow up?"

I was taught that candles are like house cats—domesticated versions of something wild and dangerous. There's no way to know how much of that killer instinct lurks in the darkness. I used to think the house-burning paranoia was the result of some upper-middle-class fear regarding the potential destruction of a half-million-dollar Westchester house the size of a matchbox. But then I realized the fear stemmed from something far less complex: we're not used to fire. Candles are a staple of Judaic existence and, like many suburban residents before us, we're pretty bad Jews.

Over the years, Judaism has become less of an ethic and more of a vaccination for our family. Aside from the biannual fireplace usage, candles only come out for Hanukah or to represent the dead. As a child, and even now if I'm home for it, a real gloom descends as we light the candles and everyone is silently reminded of how religiously inadequate we are during the rest of the year. Candles intimidate us. This makes us depressed, which makes us resent our depression, which only makes us feel more guilty. Which is its own typically Jewish experience.

I am currently in possession of my grandmother's menorah and imagine I will stay in possession of it for as long as I'd like. In my family, where the Hanukah prayer was said at Alvin and the

Chipmunks speed, it's like saying I have my grandmother's shoehorn.

But taking Hanukah lightly is not really what makes us bad Jews. I don't think God even actually knows when Hanukah starts. I'm pretty sure we rent Him out to the Catholics for the month of December and retrieve him for Yom Kippur, Rosh Hashanah, and other celebrations not based on milk chocolate and fluorescent wax. What makes us bad Jews is that we had a humongous Christmas tree throughout my formative years. It was our first real step into the latter side of Judeo-Christianity. When I tell people now that we had a Christmas tree, they ask me if both my parents are Jewish. Yes, both. "Okay then, did you ever consider the Hanukah bush?" Clearly these people have never met my father, whose own religious philosophy went something like: Why borrow a holiday when you can steal it?

And steal it he did. But in the only way he knew how: meticulously. Growing up, any project conducted under my father's watch was done with a simultaneous grand vision and attention to detail that bordered on the insane. In third grade I had to make a diorama about the Inuit. I showed up to school with a Plexiglas case that housed an igloo made from nail-filed sugar cubes and a battery-powered fan that created dry ice. It was difficult to claim I had created a functioning arctic biosphere on my own, given that long division was a struggle. So imagine then, if you will, the kind of Christmas tree we're talking about. One year, my father managed to defile a tree to the point of wrapping two whole packages of lights around the trunk.

It wasn't always that way. Both my parents' parents were Jewish. None more so than my father's mother. She raised her boys in Brighton Beach. Before that, she lived on Orchard Street on the Lower East Side of Manhattan, where she was proposed to by Zero Mostel. She was a socialist. She loved *The Golden Girls*. Ed Koch came to her funeral. When she died, she insisted on being buried in red, the logic being that God would make her an exception among the Jews—if she was going to Hell, she at least wanted to be dressed for it.

It wasn't until high school that I realized my grandmother wasn't actually "Jewish Jewish" at all, at least not by the time I came into existence. Apparently, in a parallel universe on the other side of town, a private school was being conducted called Solomon Schechter. Most of these kids merged into public school after eighth grade. They were fluent in Hebrew. They had been bar mitzvahed. I couldn't drink Manischewitz without throwing up.

Here, at the tender age of fourteen, I was about to find out the difference between being a religious Jew and a "lax" Jew.

Being a "lax" Jew used to refer to the distance between one's beliefs and one's diligence in practicing those beliefs. It was defined by a lack of fervor. But even now, at social gatherings, I effortlessly define myself as a "lax Jew," as if the "lax" carries as much official weight as the "Jew." In a way it does. Like Religious Reaganomics, Lax Judaism is a trickle-down faith in its own right and upon closer examination is actually a misnomer. You can't fall away from something if you were never there in the first place. It's the difference between jumping off a cliff and passing out where you stand. For the lax Jew, it's not a personal soul-dividing betrayal to eat on Yom Kippur. No one expects you to be able to spell "yarmulke." I played the flute for exactly one day in fourth grade, so the logic behind me being a "lax" Jew would also have me being a lax flute player. For better or worse, this phenomenon seems to be ours and ours alone. Never do we see a man with only two wives and say: lax Mormon.

The Schecter kids were hard-core Jews and I was fascinated by them the same way I would later be fascinated by the Choate- and Exeter-raised students at college. I had certain ideas about private school people. I thought they were good in everything they did. I thought they ate right and woke up before their alarm clocks went off and played the viola. I was legitimately confused to find they were delinquents-in-training like the rest of us. Perhaps they had always planned to drink and smoke up and blare gangsta rap from their Jettas. It started to occur to me that maybe religious practice was like tennis practice. You play up, depending on who's on the other side of the net. Which meant that we were dragging these kids down.

Meanwhile, I was hardly playing up myself. My new religious friends were surprised that I didn't attend Hebrew school but they were flat-out shocked that I had never gone to a Jewish-themed summer camp. "Jew camp," as it was unfortunately dubbed, was huge. I have no idea how Jewish these camps get, but since we're talking about Westchester, they're probably more intense than those in North Dakota. But how? Making kosher s'mores? Crafting dreidels out of Fimo? Dropping *both* skis and walking on water? It remains a mystery to me.

For eight consecutive years, I spent my summers all but forgetting I was ever Jewish. I went to a camp that was not only in New England but a place where we sang the Lord's Prayer before breakfast. Having never said—and certainly never sung—the prayer before or since, just humming the tune reminds me of the sound of 120 girls in a mess hall. I can still hear them clinking their spoons into bowls of Rice Krispies. I can still see them armed with bottles of strawberry Quik and miniature plastic steins of powdered lemonade, the loot of freshly opened care packages. I have subsequently discovered that my parents had no idea it was a Christian-based camp. Only a few states away, camp was defining their daughter's religious beliefs and they didn't have a clue. It wasn't Bible camp but it was closer than it had any right to be.

It is important to understand how steeped in bizarre tradition summer camp is, so that when Jesus slips in there, he goes almost unnoticed. Think of a zany romantic comedy in which a woman mistakenly swallows her engagement ring because it was cleverly tucked in her chocolate soufflé. This is how I swallowed Christianity. My summer camp inspired the kind of intense psychotic loyalty and bonding normally catalyzed by negative experiences—plane crashes, hostage situations, concentration camps. It was an idyllic lakeside compound in rural New Hampshire, and I bawled my eyes out at the end of each summer when I had to leave it. Those girls and I were in the shit together. When I was twelve, I wrote in a journal that I did not want to be buried in a Jewish cemetery. Instead I wanted to be cremated, my ashes scattered in the stream that ran through the grounds.

It's not that we didn't do normal camp things: I learned archery, sailing, poison ivy identification, what it feels like to get your front tooth knocked out by a tether ball. But behind this summertime merriment was a society of malleable little girls learning a bizarre series of hymnals and faux Native American chants. Not uncommon for the region, the camp's theme was Native American—the cabins had Native American names, the dining hall had Native American decorations, and we wore feathers in our braids and painted our faces for capture the flag. It was about as decent a tribute to a culture as a Hanukah bush. But mimicking Native American tradition was only one piece of it. We also folded the American flag military-style every night, tied the rope a certain way, and wore uniforms from the army-navy surplus store while calling our counselors "Miss." It was a clusterfuck of ritual.

On Sunday nights we had vespers, where we lit candles and sang folk songs with titles like "The Lord Loves a Strong Swimmer" and "All God's Critters Got a Place in the Choir," a banjo going full-country speed in the background. "All God's Critters" was a song with such complexity that to sing it was to congratulate yourself on knowing the words. Much like "We Didn't Start the Fire," which I had never mastered back in the real world. It even had *Grease*-like matching hand motions.

> *All God's critters got a place in the choir*
> *Some sing low, some sing higher*
> *Some sing out loud on the telephone wire*

And some just clap their hands, or paws
Or anything they got now

Listen to the bass, it's the one on the bottom
Where the bullfrog croaks and the hippopotamus
Moans and groans with a big to-do
The old cow just goes "Moo"
MOOOOO

The dog and the cat pick up the middle
While the honeybee hums and the cricket fiddles
The donkey brays and the pony neighs
And the old coyote howls

And we'd all "Howwwl" and go to sleep, unconsciousness being the only acceptable break from song. The next morning, awoken by a bugle recording over the loudspeaker, we'd sing ABBA's altered-for-your-girlhood "I Have a Dream." Instead of:

I believe in angels
When I know the time is right for me
I'll cross the stream—have a dream

We sang:

I believe in Wa-klo
'Cause I know the place is right for me
In woods and streams—I've found my dreams.

And then we'd pray. We were brainwashed and we loved it. Every Saturday night the entire camp marched into a clearing in the woods, where we lit a gigantic bonfire. Four girls were selected each week to dip torches into the crackling fireball. Each torch represented a moral category at which we aimed to excel: Friendship, Cleanliness, Sportsmanship, and Love. What they really were were long sticks we'd find in the woods the evening before. We'd wrap the ends in extra-large overnight maxi pads and roast them in the flames as we said our prayers. Then we'd hold them above our heads, imagining how embarrassing it would be to explain that one's death—or worse, one's disfigurement—came from a flaming maxi pad to the face.

Looking back, this seems like a self-hating ritual for an all-girls camp. Bras, okay, they have a political history. But maxi pads? Alas, we were caught in the moment, incinerating the practical evidence of being women in order to stay girls forever. Despite an upbringing that didn't allow for much flaming outdoor ritual, I was soon torching feminine products with the best of them.

Meanwhile, the incorporation of Jesus and Native American folktales seemed more normal with each passing year. Sometimes I wondered if Jesus lived, and during those times I came to believe that he was God's son. I decided to keep my newfound revelation from my parents. Here were these people who would gather me at the end of each summer, impervious to my hysterics about leaving camp and preoccupied with the coming school year. They wouldn't "get" Jesus. I had found him and they weren't even looking for him.

I thought perhaps I was mistakenly born into the Jews anyway. I don't look especially Jewish. This is always an awkward social observation. No one in his or her right mind would ever tell a biracial girl, "Funny, you don't look black." And here I am, one hundred percent Jewish, and people say: Really?

And I say: Really.

And they say: You don't look Jewish *at all*.

At which point I usually clap my hands and rub them together, like I'm off to man the grill, and say, "Great! Guess that means I would have had a decent shot at surviving the Holocaust!"

But that's now. At camp, I accepted this comment as a compliment. This was very dangerous for a kid like me, who was hanging on to her Judaism by a tzit-tzit thread as it was. I had no rituals that resembled "religious" at home. I had patterns—walking the dog, brushing my teeth, flushing my sister's bite plate down the toilet. And I had talismans—stuffed animals, tie-dyed slouch socks, an awesome sticker collection. But never did they overlap.

I came close to building my own theological infrastructure at the ripe age of seven, when I memorized a series of words: Sky, Blankey, Speech, Kim. I said them over and over again, like a mantra. I would say them under my breath when I was frightened or rendered dizzy by a Tilt-a-Whirl. Skyblankeyspeechkim.

Our Siamese cat, who we loved so much he survived on mass affection and insulin injections until I was twenty-five, was called Skyler. Skyler used to curl up in my pink blankey, which I still have. When I started middle school, my mother began encouraging me to get rid of it. What are you going to do, take that thing to college? When I started college, she said, What are you going to do, have it in bed with you and your husband one day? Meanwhile, "speech" was when I'd line my stuffed animals up after my parents had tucked me in and talk to them about the day's events. Skyler would be invited to these sophisticated salons as well and I'd scratch his ears and ponder running away from home, love, sex, death, and how cool it would be if I was a spy or mermaid or both and came to school as a spy-maid one morning.

Then there was Kim, the closest thing I had to God before I went to camp and discovered Jesus. Kim was my invisible friend. Except that she wasn't. I never spoke to her, never talked about her to anyone. All I did was name her and decide she was there. I forgot her at home or at school. If she had been a Tamagotchi, her little electronic soul would have died of neglect. I have no idea what she looked like. What I did know was that little kids were supposed to have invisible friends. The abnormal action of relating to the invisible was so encouraged by child psychologists that I felt abnormal not having one of my own.

So there we were: the Cat, the Blankey, and the Invisible Spirit.

I hadn't thought of any of this until a year ago when I was on a flight and the complimentary blanket was called a "sky blanket." I said it involuntarily: Sky, Blankey, Speech, Kim. I had almost forgotten. It's so clear to me now: the memorizing of a fake prayer, the symbolization of objects, the struggle to relate to the invisible—I needed a religion. I was lost. I was in a remote Native American–themed chick commune in New Hampshire. I was in danger.

The pinnacle of said danger came during the last week of July. That's when we had "Christmas" and I—a nine-year-old Jew—

found myself catching the Christmastime spirit. We had Hanukah, too, of course—the camp directors lit a menorah for eight nights and put it on their table in the mess hall, which was called Cracker Barrel. Years later, when I discovered that there was a national restaurant chain by the same name, I became highly irritated that a piece of my cultish sanctuary was available to every trucker on I-95. If you ask my fellow ex-campers, I'd bet good money they had the same reaction. That's the kind of place this was.

Just like in real time, Hanukah began a week or so before Christmas. And, just like in real time, it served as more of a signifier that Christmas was coming than as a holiday unto itself. The camp's directors put a couple of electronic menorahs—the Jewish equivalent to a string of Budweiser cans—in the dining hall. Still, they were easy to miss. One of the bigger mistakes the Jews ever made was having these skinny candles represent Hanukah. Because that's what happened. It became a thin holiday, while Christmas has a whole glazed ham on its bones. Techni cally we have more of a right to our candles than, say, a Douglas fir—dressed in drag and humiliated with fairy lights—repre-sents the birth of Christ. There is a direct correlation with the story of Hanukah and the long-burning oil (I think Eastern Mountain Sports sells it to campers now). Yet, was there a giant pine tree in the middle of the desert on Jesus's birthday? "Here, Jesus," says Joseph, "I saw this and thought of you."

But oh, to have Christmas in July! We lived all summer for it. Christmas consisted of seven days of Secret Santa (during which I invariably got the smelly kid who loved to give "crafts" or had to give to one of the European girls who lacked the palate for Fun

Dip). The week ended with the Christmas play that Sunday. The play told the story of the life of Christ, complete with hay from the horse stables, bunnies from the barn, and fake blood from Halloween in June. We were allowed to forgo our uniforms and come to the play in flannel pajamas and Totes Toasties socks. Afterward we sang Lord-praising carols and lit more candles than usual, which should have made me extremely nervous. All those brown pine needles and birch benches . . . But it didn't. I figured Jesus would protect me.

Then we drank hot chocolate and exchanged our final gifts, purchased during rare excursions into civilization. These would be matching pajama sets or clever coffee mugs filled with candy and pencils. Across the bustling room, a profoundly good-natured teenager from Madrid gave her own Game Boy and a bottle of Chanel Number 5 as her final gift. I accepted my pipe cleaner anklet as graciously as possible. It was the Christian thing to do.

In 1989, the summer I turned ten, there was a girl who lived in my cabin, a girl from Darien, Connecticut, with long wavy blond hair, who was set to play Mary in the Christmas play. She had also been the recipient of the Madrid girl's gift, the Secret Santa jackpot. Perhaps if I'd had God in my life growing up I would have been able to understand the total and complete unfairness of the universe rewarding mean girls. I had befriended other wavy blond bunkmates before, but this girl was new to camp and I hated her on sight. She used to stand in the middle of the cabin and flip her hair upside down, combing it from the neck down, a habit which I found bizarrely unsanitary. She wore pearl earrings while swimming in the lake and slept beneath a Ralph Lauren comforter. She used Skin So Soft instead of Off!, and wore Esprit bathing suits instead of the regulation army-navy surplus store ones. In her monogrammed Caboodle, she had a sticker collection that would make grown women weep. She was mean to the ugly girls, the flat-chested girls, and most of the Spanish girls (not a wise move, as one of them would turn out to be the niece of that country's president). She went to a boarding school in Connecticut, and I knew that she represented the end of my childhood.

Within the next few years, the camp would double the cost of an eight-week stay. Then they would do away with the regulation uniforms and puke green one-piece swimsuits of which we all owned three (like a troupe of Smurfettes with the same dress on every hanger). Eventually, campers would be allowed to watch television, call home, and bare their midriffs. Girls would no longer be asked to address their counselors as "Miss," cell phones would blink in the night along with the lightning bugs, and Field Day would be recorded live for the new website.

One thing would remain the same: the powerful popularity of blondes. My being flat in the chest and poofy on the head did not win me points with the Girl from Darien. And points with her suddenly seemed more valuable than the colored feathers we earned for treading water. Not only did she have a steady boyfriend, she had tongue-kissed him. A modeling scout had approached her in the Stamford mall and asked her to model for Guess Jeans but her mother said she was too young. If not for that, we would have all seen her before we met her.

One night, as we lay awake in our bunks, the Girl from Darien told us a story about her mother, who, while attending the University of Oklahoma, had met a Jewish girl and asked her if she had horns. She expressed a ten-year-old's outrage at the narrow-mindedness of the world. Her frankness was met with commiseration in the dark and a glee at how adult our conversation was. My mind spun. I had no idea that people thought Jews had horns. Where I came from, Jews had good grades and BMWs. I would have just as soon asked the Girl from Darien if she had wings. I also didn't know why having horns was an insult. Unicorns had horns and they were the coolest creatures in existence. What I did know was that this girl was far too proud of her tale of injustice.

My father did this sometimes, so I recognized it—a tweaked-out kind of racism in which one is abnormally accepting of others simply *because* they're different. To this day, he has a keen interest in how my black and gay friends are doing. He loves seeing old Chinese men and Mexican babies. Once, at a local Indian restaurant, my mother asked the waiter how to pronounce a dish. At which point Dad chimed in with, "He doesn't know, Derry! Do you have any idea how many dialects there are in India? Millions!" It was one of those moments when I wished to be better educated or fluent in an obscure language. "They're not called dialects, Dad, they're called [insert foreign word I don't know]. And there are only [insert number I don't know] of them."

Lying there in the chilly New Hampshire night, wrapping my Blankey around my hands like a muff, I became prickly on behalf of my former religion and its keratin-faced adherents.

"I don't think the Jews need our pity," I whispered into the rafters. "I don't think anyone who has seen me would believe I have horns either."

"Everyone needs pity," the Girl from Darien replied, whip smart, "and I'm not just saying that because I believe in God."

I mumbled, "Skyblankeyspeechkim," and rolled over in my squeaky bunk. Did girls like her not have summer homes or Swiss Alps to terrorize? I wanted her to leave my humble hamlet of goodness. One week later, I got my wish. It was just before the Christmas play and I was playing a strenuous game of Ping-Pong when word came that the Girl from Darien had slammed into a dock while waterskiing, broken her toe, and had to be taken to the hospital in Keene. Her parents picked her up from the ER and took her with them on vacation in Bermuda rather than returning her to a world of mothballs and communal showers. In a twist worthy of *Showgirls*, I wound up taking her role as Mary, the lead in the big Christmas play. The religious significance was insignificant. My nervousness stemmed from the fact that the girl who played Mary was always blond. Also, the only other time I had appeared on the camp's stage was the year before, when I had "choreographed" a dance to Belinda Carlisle's "Heaven Is a Place on Earth" and leapt around stage in stirrup pants until the tape mercifully faded to silence.

Being Mary would require me to memorize a few more lines than that of my prior character, a sheep. I waited in the open air backstage with the wise women, giggling and getting bit by mosquitoes. I missed my cue to enter, but Joseph (whose actual name was Josephine) pulled me by the arm while we mumbled our lines and wandered around stage like drunken homeless people. After being turned away from the inn, Joseph and I settled on a pile of center stage hay and curled up beneath a giant crucifix some girls had made in woodshop. And then I gave birth to Jesus.

Shortly after, the Girl from Darien returned to us. Metallic WELCOME letters hung from the rafter above her bunk. SweeTarts and FireBalls, Starburst and Dum-Dums lay waiting to be eaten on her pinstriped pillow. It was only because I returned early to the cabin—after a minor altercation between some lake water and my nasal passages—that I came upon this display. I squeaked short in my flip-flops. I stole an unkosher watermelon Starburst from her pillow, then flopped down on my bed and ate in celebration with myself. Had I known the plague about to befall the camp, I would have taken two.

Starting with our cabin, a few scalps in our bunk began to get scratched. Then the whole cabin. Then our whole area of camp. A lice epidemic had broken out. The Girl from Darien's days of casual hair brushing in the middle of the room were numbered. Apparently we all misunderstood—she had not fled to Bermuda but somewhere near Bali. A remote communal-living island with personal palm boys but a poor laundering system. We threw out all our combs and scrunchies. Like the Gestapo, the camp directors came in the middle of the night. They took our hair towels, drove them away on golf carts, and set them ablaze in a field somewhere. The last week of camp, the Girl from Darien hugged me good-bye and said she was sure I made a "fine" Mary. She pressed that waterfall of an infested blond mane to mine.

"Everyone needs pity," I whispered, and hugged her back.

I was sent home with a letter, a box of special shampoo, and a plastic comb. When I got off the bus—which let us off at a Mc-Donald's on the Connecticut–New York border—I handed my mother the note. I was petrified. If there was a God in her house, it was the God of Hygiene. She was furious. Since the age of two, any illness was treated as something that was done to me. I may as well have marched across the parking lot with a black eye.

I had to get rid of a lot of my lice-ridden childhood icons after that summer, including my felt archery champion patch, my "Native American" feathered headdress, and an amiable stuffed rabbit named Bruce, whose hobbies included warding off ghosts and being thrown at snoring girls. I was also forced to throw away the candle that I had used in vespers, through no fault of the candle itself, but the birchwood holder it came in, which was "probably full of bugs and mildew." I hid my Blankey.

I was upset. I felt lost. I felt itchy. Camp was over and I was back in Westchester, where everything meaningful was gone. My mother, high on Nix fumes and annoyed from triple washing all my sheets, pulled my Mary costume out of my camp regulation duffel bag and examined it carefully. She pinched the lace collar between her fingers and, after some time, sniffed it. The scent of mothballs filled the room.

"What the fuck is this?"

I had written her about my role in the play and she had been proud, even found it funny, but seeing physical evidence of it was different. I had never heard her curse before—at least not with such venom and not without slapping her hand over her mouth immediately afterward. It wasn't the kind of rage I would have chosen for her, as I knew it wasn't on my behalf. It had no traces of shame or nostalgia or regret. It did not say, "This has gone too far," or, "My child could grow up to become a fanatical but vital leader of the Christian right. Whatever shall I do?" It was instead simpler than that, an in-the-moment disgust that did not reflect any changes to come. We would still be bad Jews. We would still have a Christmas tree with favorite ornaments. We would still feast like Catholics on the Christmas Yule log with plastic reindeer prancing through icing. We would have the biggest tree on the block, and bagels and lox the next day, and light Hanukah candles as carefully as surgeons to the tune of a prayer we barely knew. But this costume was not us.

She threw it at me. "Toss it," she said, moving on to my socks and underwear with a pair of salad tongs. "Now."

I walked obediently toward the garbage, keeping my eyes fixed on my mother. She systematically and unemotionally dismantled a summer's worth of grass-stained clothes, leaky sunscreen bottles, and a cardboard snowflake with loosely glued glitter that fell in slow motion. Her fingers sparkled like an angel's as she wiped them clean on her jeans. And for the first time, I found God.

THE URSULA COOKIE

There is a point in most abusive relationships when it occurs to the beaten party that they are guilty of putting their face in the way of someone else's fist. The speed that sucker was going, it was bound to hit someone, so why not you? You're qualified. Why not be the first in line for a grade-A white-collar beatdown? Pack up your college degree and camp out in your new suit the night before your interview. Pitch a tent using a Montblanc as the pole and watermarked résumés for walls. When your future boss comes into the office, greeting the downtrodden mouse of an assistant you hope to replace with an "Any messages *now?*" let yourself scream inside: "Pick me! Punch me! Thank you, ma'am, may I have another?!" Pay your dues like a Girl Scout and crumble like a thin mint. I'll tell you why not.

By the time I graduated, I had groomed myself into an ideal liberal-arts worker bee with a pitch-perfect buzz for magazine publishing. I had more magazine internships under my belt than I had actual belts. My first was for *Westchester Family* magazine, located in the office space above a bicycle repair shop in Mamaroneck. The hours I logged in there were some of the more useless of my life. Which is really saying something. I remember almost nothing of my experience except for the tray of inexplicably unwrapped cherry frosted Pop-Tarts in the office kitchen and the one article they allowed me to write all summer: a two-hundred-word reportage masterpiece on a teen fashion show at Macy's. In it, I attempted to explore the seedy underbelly of thirteen-year-old runway models, all of whom had better skin and better social lives than I did. What came out went something like: Shoulder pads. All bad?

Before long, I moved on to simultaneously bigger and skinnier things. Like some heartless family "forgetting" to bring their mangy cat with them when they moved, I quickly dropped *Westchester Family* off my résumé as soon as I had something with national cachet and a 212 area code to replace it. Over the course of three summer internships in Manhattan I filed articles, ran errands, mastered the electric hole puncher, transcribed interviews that took place on windy sailboats, and gave myself more than one paper cut in that little stretch of webbing between one's thumb and one's index finger. I had gone on wild mousse chases for mauve mascara at one publication and a synonym for "decoupage" at another. I had been drooled on by sleeping Metro North commuters in neckties. I had blisters on my feet and Frederic Fekkai in my hair. Ladies and gentlemen: I had blown on another woman's tea.

And this merely accounts for my jobs that were illuminated by fluorescent bulbs. It says nothing of my illustrious mall career at various high-end clothing retailers, places where there's an eternal snobbery tug-of-war between customer and employee. Nor have I mentioned my brief stint as a stylist to my neighbor's cats or my even briefer stint as a tennis coach to prepubescent teens, popping out the phrase "shake hands with the racquet" with the consistency of a ball machine.

Yet despite my self-grooming for fashion magazines, or perhaps because of it, I knew two things: (1) there is no synonym for "decoupage" and (2) I wanted out as fast as possible when it came time for my first job.

It's not that I didn't want to learn about thickening vs. lengthening mascara, because truly, I did. My mother, bless her heart, had taught me many life skills but knowing the difference between matte and powder foundation was not among them. But what I realized was that magazines would be ruined for me if I made them my life. I would no longer be able to enjoy *Vogue* on the train if I associated its creation with my commute. Books, however, seemed a more indestructible passion. I read. I was a reader. "Are you a big reader?" the headhunters would say, squinting their eyes from their Midtown East cubicle farms. Oh, big. And with that, I shifted my focus away from the notoriously cold and calculating world of glossy mastheads and back to the warm, welcoming womb of bound prose. I was ready for my true calling. I was ready for a career in book publishing. I could smell the glue already.

* * *

The first time I saw Ursula she came rushing past me with two large canvas bags slung over each shoulder, holding a full-sized floor lamp by its neck. The tassels on the shade vibrated and the plug dragged behind her like a small obedient dog. I sat invisibly in the waiting room of the strangely old-fashioned seven-person office that would become my home for the next year or so. The office secretary, Lenore, nodded at me and I followed the tail of the lamp down the hall and into Ursula's office. It looked like the cover shot for some gag book on how not to feng shui your home. Stacks of manuscripts formed tiny forts around smaller stacks of recently published books. These in turn hid untold treasures, perhaps in the form of loose contracts or petrified rubber bands that had not seen the sunlight through the unwashed windows since the 1970s. It was the kind of room that you look at and think, simply: forensics. I was smitten with every asthma-inducing bit of it. The search for one's first professional job is not unlike a magical love potion: when one wants to fall in love with the next thing one sees, one generally does.

Ursula asked me to sit down as she pulled manuscript after manuscript out of the bags. It was as if the *Paris Review* had a clown car and she had rented it. For the grand finale, she pulled out a hand-painted vase with an image of the Mona Lisa holding a rose in her teeth.

"Isn't it terrific?" she said. "Flea market."

Then she plopped down in her old leather chair, smiled, and said: "So."

32

We talked for over two hours and I fell in love with her. And she fell in love with me back. She stopped picking up the phone. We discussed the state of book publishing, the state of Iowa, the seminal decades for the art of the short story. We were both Leos and we both had a penchant for bad Mexican food. Better still, she was the exact same age as my mother and her husband was the exact same age as my father. She talked faster than I did, laughed at everything I said, and called me "a good egg." Eventually I became so comfortable that when she asked me how my friends would describe me, I said, "Oh, you know, a loose cannon"—using air quotes—"no, but seriously . . ."

If book publishing was this woman, then book publishing was for me. I felt almost Calvinistically destined to be her assistant. This was a woman who would take me under her wing. This was a woman who needed someone to understand her and anticipate her needs. This was a woman who needed her plants watered. I could do these things. When I got home from the interview she had already called, brimming with compliments and offering me the job.

Sarah was the name of the assistant I replaced. She stayed for two days to train me before going back to grad school to become a prison psychologist studying the calming effects of Chopin on mass murderers. Those two days were dreamy and simple. I was the storefront and Sarah was the supply room. Every time Ursula asked me a question, I went back and asked Sarah, who provided me with the answer. On Sarah's last day, Ursula took us out to lunch, where my eagerness to please was an early-onset disease. I intentionally left Sarah in the dust during a conversation about Virginia Woolf simply because I happened to have written my senior thesis on the woman. I figured, what did it matter? I was only competing against myself and, really, she was already gone. By Friday the only sign Sarah had sat in the same chair for two years was a postcard of Alcatraz tacked to the wall, her initials on Ursula's letters, and a single sheet of vital phone numbers as if I were inheriting an incontinent house pet.

At this point I feel I would be remiss to not mention the prevalence of a specific kind of person who enters the field of book publishing. This is the English lit major who never should have left academia, a genius who has read all of V. S. Naipaul but can't photocopy title pages right side up. This person is very thin, possibly vegan, probably Ivy League. He or she feels as if answering the phone in a chipper voice is a form of legalized prostitution. He or she has a single quirky and defining fashion piece, usually red or black, and waxes poetic about typewriters and the British, having never truly known either. Regardless of sex, they all want to be David Foster Wallace when they grow up.

I was not this person. My stint as a vegan was brief, as was my tolerance for postcolonial Indian literature. Plus I had a cast-iron upper-middle-class work ethic that was akin to a superpower. Or at least an electric fence—one that simply wouldn't let me deny my basic skills as a glorified secretary. Nothing was beneath me but the sidewalk. There was no fax machine I couldn't operate on sight. No database I couldn't navigate through. No letter of the alphabet I couldn't file under. Which is why I was just as surprised as Ursula the first time I lost a phone message. I told Ursula the name of someone important who had called while she was in a meeting, but when I went to retrieve the piece of paper, it had vanished. I don't know where it went. Maybe the foreign rights elves took it, I don't know. I would suspect sabotage, but aside from Ursula I was the youngest person in the office, by approximately 167 years, and I just didn't think the others had it in them. I stood in her doorway, my head hung low. She sighed and rolled her eyes.

"I swear," she said, "I don't know what goes through your head sometimes."

I looked up, startled. Sometimes? We were on week two. Surely, she must be talking to herself. I sloughed it off. But soon the scolding became unsloughable.

Take the letters, for example. It was officially the new millennium, but Ursula would write all her letters by hand, often on the backs of restaurant receipts. I'd spend hours attempting to type them into legibility, holding them at various lengths from my face. I would occasionally be able to make out an otherwise unintelligible word from its context but would employ my isolated interpretation of her scrawl when typing the letter. This, in the vain hope that she would write more clearly next time.

"Weasel? Why the hell would I ask for something by Weasel of next year?" She'd shove the paper back into my palm.

Then there was the endless ghostly parade of missing objects. At least once a day Ursula would lose something and send me running around the office looking for it, firing the start gun of

"You better find it or . . ." And off I went, not wanting to stick around for the rest of that sentence. When I would invariably come up empty-handed, she would say, "Oh, that? I actually found that on my desk hours ago."

What was happening? This woman I had so admired (albeit prematurely), this purloiner of my first job virginity, turned scathing. Some people do yoga in the morning; Ursula gave looks so stern I believe she burned calories creating them. When had I become no better than a haughty vegan Anglophile? It was all so unfair: I had never even *read* David Foster Wallace. I was a good egg, but I guess you can't make an omelet without breaking a few.

Before working for Ursula, I'd never had difficulty retaining information, but suddenly I was so petrified of messing up that the fear blocked all my memory pores. It didn't take long for me to become precisely what she thought I was: a lousy assistant. Everything I touched turned to shit. I had not known the answers to one too many of her rapid-fire questions and now her trust was broken. I began losing things, misfiling them, sending out the wrong versions of them. The phone would ring, and she'd come popping out of her office like a prairie dog to watch me answer it. Six months had gone by when she stopped scolding and started throwing. Pens, junk mail, a blessedly unbound four-hundred-page manuscript—whatever happened to be in her hand at the time sailed in the general direction of my head. I became acutely aware that, in an office environment, people are almost always holding something. When you screw up as much as I did, it's an unavoidable observation. There was nothing I could do except surreptitiously hide the letter openers.

To this day, I have never cried at the office. There was one instance, however, in which I cried *near* it. After a particularly rough heart-to-heart with Ursula after I'd sent something out via FedEx instead of UPS, it was unsubtly suggested that I find another industry in which to work. I got out on the street and started crying the kind of hysterical tears made justifiable only by turning off one's cell phone, putting it to the ear, and pretend-ing to be told of a death in the family. A few blocks later, I ducked into a public atrium and turned my phone back on. I called my sister, a gifted jewelry designer, successful businesswoman, and functioning member of society. Lowering my voice to prevent it from echoing, I found myself glossing over the shameful details. Having dried my tears blocks before, it now seemed anticlimactic to complain. All that came out was that I was dissatisfied with my work situation and that I had broken the Xerox machine. My sis-ter advised me to stick with it. This was only my first job. Hadn't I ever heard of paying my dues?

Around this time my precious work ethic began to atrophy in earnest and—truth be told—it has never returned. A basic affin-ity for office work may appear expendable to most. But I was a good girl from the suburbs, where self-worth was color-coded and bound and crazy-glued into a diorama. Yet when the phone in Ursula's office would ring, I'd run to the bathroom to avoid picking it up. I'd run to the bathroom in general. As a break I'd indulge myself by locking the main door to the ladies' room, sit-ting on the radiator, and breathing. I was, in fact, in that very spot when it dawned on me that Sarah had opted to spend the rest of her life in America's most violent prisons rather than work another day for Ursula. Once Ursula said to me, almost as a point of fascination, "You sit out there all day and I have no idea what you're doing." I wish I could have answered her. E-mail had not yet made its way to the few office computers, nor had the Internet. Mostly I was staring at the plastic bumps on my coffee lid, blurring my vision to make them turn from "cream," "black," and "decaf" to "laid off," "demoted," and "fired."

Over and over I tried to comprehend how things had taken such an acerbic turn. I was a splendid photocopier! I was a finder, not a loser! Dozens, perhaps even as many as thirty, of America's youth had a better forehand grip because of me. Besides, having tasted the rarefied air of the lofty literary world, I couldn't go back to shoulder pads and mascara. I sought solace in the receptionist, Lenore, who would tell me that she had seen worse assistants than me. Like a kid demanding her favorite fairy tale before bedtime, I'd repeatedly make her tell me about the dreadful assistant who lasted only a month. About how she was fired for incompetence, cast out of the kingdom of literature, and was now working in textbook publishing in Scranton.

Having never had another first job, I didn't know enough to quit. As the weeks rolled by, I remained convinced that I could fix the situation. Just when I was at my most unmotivated and depressed, I would imagine what things would be like if Ursula knew me in a different context. She was so wonderful to anyone who was not me. I couldn't shake the feeling that in a different world I would be her favorite neighbor or niece. Perhaps when her own daughter grew up she could focus all that marvelously passive aggression on her own spawn, saying things like, "Why can't you be more like Sloane?" or, "If you're doing a report on *The Taming of the Shrew,* perhaps we should call Sloane. I know she wrote quite the extensive tome on Shakespeare's early work, but it might be hard for you to read since her primary medium at the time was finger paint."

I was in a relationship that was going south and going there fast, but if I could just get my partner to see me how she used to—to fall in love with me all over again—everything would be okay. Every morning I would vow to work harder, and every morning something would go wrong. Ursula would insist she'd told me something she hadn't. Or, worse, some task would be poorly executed (by me) and Ursula would give me a look indicating that she would like to do some executing of her own. Soon even Lenore couldn't help herself. "I've never seen her so pissed before," or, "I'm buying you earplugs for Christmas." I was the most easily deflated person on the planet. Ursula's husband would drop by the office on occasion and give me indiscernible looks. If it was a good day, I would think they were empathetic. Who knew what it was to live under these masochistically matriarchal conditions better than he! If it was a bad day, they would roughly translate to, "So you're the idiot."

The funny thing was, I was already in a relationship. It was my first real postcollege relationship, with an extraordinarily tall man who was a pot dealer by night and a paralegal at a major law firm by day. He used to lock the doors to abandoned offices and take unwieldy naps under the desks with his legs sticking out. Or he'd call me.

He expressed concern about the change in my personality.

"I've never seen you so . . ."

"What? So what?" I was down to a single gear: defensive.

"Mousy."

"I'm not mousy. I don't even know what that means."

But it was true. Not only was I becoming a mousy assistant, I was becoming a mousy person. My backstabbing behavior with Sarah at that first lunch had become exacerbated. I was incredibly disloyal. The few times Ursula spoke to me anymore, she'd complain about Lenore.

"She gets in here at ten o'clock with her disgusting breakfast sandwiches and then she doesn't begin working for another hour."

I would roll my eyes in sympathetic disgust, sliding a book over my cheese croissant.

The one thing I did right the entire year was to write a typo-free letter to the U.S. Postal Service. Ursula summoned me into her office and explained in great detail that she had ordered stamps—an act which itself seemed a totally irrational, above-and-beyond enterprise, as it was simple enough to sneak one's personal utility bills in with the office mail. On top of which, I have never known anyone who orders stamps before. Such foresight seemed reserved for Target-shopping Midwesterners and people who pressed their own flowers. It was not for women who said things like "some people are despicable idiots" before nine A.M., referring to the coffee cart man.

No matter, she saw me as an ally. When she called someone else a name, I took it as a personal compliment. Apparently the "morons" at the post office (them, not me!) had screwed over the wrong woman by sending her a row fewer stamps than she paid for. She had made several maddening phone calls in which she had been put on hold and led down a primrose path of automated options. Now it was my job to "level with them."

I sat at my desk and focused all my energy into being Ursula. Who is this woman? What's her motivation? I thought about the massive *Mommy Dearest*–sized gap I perceived between what she let me see and what she let the world see. I thought about the way she'd come back from a business lunch with the smile still on her face, the way she'd laugh out loud on the phone or politely ask people for things, and the way all of her turned to stone when I walked into a room. And then I began to feel that a gap was the wrong image.

This whole time I had imagined her as a boss with a typically terrifying split personality, a woman whose bad side you'd never want to get on. In stepping into her head, however briefly, I realized that the two Ursulas were connected. It was all one big frantic personality and it never went away. I would never get on her good side because there was no good side.

The letter was perfect. Reasonable but firm, professional but conversational. Ursula even told me so, taking on the pleasantly surprised tone of a mother whose child had not wet the bed. A week later the extra row of stamps arrived in their wax paper sheath. I put them on her desk. I have no idea if she found them.

Then came Christmas and, with it, overheated Metro North trains and a sprained ankle from slipping on slush in Grand Central. My boyfriend, Jimmy the Pothead Paralegal, dropped the last part of his title when he quit his day job. He was now free to sleep until noon in his apartment, which was located somewhere along the stretch of shit-stained cracked pavement on Ninth Street between Avenues B and C. This was just before the neighborhood got "cute," back when you couldn't walk from point B to point C without breathing in a couple of feces-hungry flies. I was still commuting in from Westchester where everything was insect-free and Windexed and there were always ample paper products. Even now that I live in Manhattan, I think of his apartment as an alternate reality, a sort of falling-off-the-grid vacuum where no one ever goes to bed, everyone smokes with the windows shut, roommates wake up naked on the kitchen floor for no reason, and no one does the dishes. Ever.

I stayed overnight at Jimmy's more and more. It was modern bohemian squalor at its finest and it was a million miles away from my daytimes.

Years later I would read a business book for women with a photograph of a woman in a suit on the cover. Her arms were crossed; presumably, she is the author. I didn't actually read this book so much as I saw it in a bookstore, thought it was amusing, and flipped it open. "Resist the urge to bake for your coworkers," cried the book. "You're not Betty Crocker!" Clearly this was not a title marketed to the pastry industry. I slid the book back onto the shelf, unaware of how sage that advice was. Had I known, maybe I never would have created the Ursula Cookie.

Since baking has been my one consistent hobby since pre-school, I often turn to it in times of stress. Just in time for the holidays, I had learned to make that smooth solid icing that goes on professionally decorated sugar cookies. I stayed up half the night in the kitchen, making stockings, Stars of David, triple-chocolate lumps of coal, and red circles that would have to be explained as "reindeer noses." The later into the night it got, the further I tested the boundaries of the holiday cookie milieu. It started innocently enough: flowers, stars, sailboats. I became too tired to sleep. I was despondent and I needed a vacation. Actually, I needed a whole new life, but as long as I never went to bed, I felt I could postpone waking up for my current one. Soon I was making baby pink handcuffs, coconut grim reaper sickles, and the inevitable penis cookie. I took some green food coloring and made marijuana leaves for Jimmy. I dusted them with powdered sugar to represent his increasingly varied substance habits.

At about three in the morning, covered in flour, my fingertips dyed primary colors, the idea for the Ursula Cookie came down from the heavens like the speckled spotlights in *Ghost*. Never in the history of human thought has a single notion so thoroughly undergone the "it seemed like a good idea at the time" metamor-phosis: the impulse was just a seed, still in its genius stage, when

I picked up a wad of wet flour and began pressing it into the shape of Ursula's head. When baked, the Ursula Cookie was the size of a small Frisbee. I gave her thick yellow flipped-up hair, intense green eyes, candy balls for earrings, and skin like, well, dough.

Sometimes, when you do something so marvelously idiotic, it's hard to retrace your thought processes using the functional logic now available to you. This is often referred to as "temporary insanity." I would venture to guess that I gave Ursula a cookie in her likeness to dissuade her of my total retardation. I wanted one last go at getting back into her favor, a place I felt I was mistakenly locked out of to begin with. I don't know what I was thinking.

"Is this me?" Ursula held the cookie by the corner of its Ziploc bag. I had come in at nine on the dot despite my sleepless night and pranced into her office with my present as soon as I heard her hang up the phone. In her tight pinch it looked like a piece of crime scene evidence.

I immediately realized my mistake. I was overcome with the urge to snatch the cookie out of her hands and gobble it up. Weighing my options, I decided that literally biting her head off might make things worse.

"Yes," I mumbled, my foot making circles on the taupe office carpeting. I was embarrassed to have been reduced to the level of a child, embarrassed to have given her a homemade gift, embarrassed by how suddenly and indisputably unprofessional it seemed to give one's boss a cookie in the shape of her disembodied head. But mostly I was embarrassed to have proven to her that even in the realm outside of the office, I was a failure. Had I not given her the cookie directly, she would never have been able to finger it as her own likeness in a bakery lineup. It looked nothing like her.

"Too funny," she said, and shut her door.

Later I found out that she gave it to her daughter, who ate the whole thing and spontaneously threw up from all the sweetness. After that, Ursula and I stopped speaking altogether. We silently timed it so that we took separate elevators. She forwarded me voice-mail messages and gave me instructions on Post-it Notes. I typed up my to-do list in the morning and left a marked-up version in her in-box at night. We ignored each other on the street. We went on like that until September of 2001.

Then came the lowest of the low points, as hard as it is to believe that the Ursula Cookie was not it. I found myself awake at three in the morning. Again. This time it was Jimmy's birthday and I was spending the night. Jimmy befriended a lot of people who wouldn't leave. Anywhere and ever. I could never understand this, as my parents raised me to arrive and leave everywhere early. Three of Jimmy's delinquent friends sat in the living room, chain-smoking and theorizing about how much it would actually hurt if you broke someone's jaw by making them bite a cement curb and kicking them in the back of the head. One of them was midsentence around four A.M. when I got up, went into Jimmy's room, and shut the door.

Eventually he followed me in. I was awake in his bed, which took up the majority of his bedroom. The heat was broken and I was coming down with the flu. Jimmy began mumbling in his sleep. After fruitlessly trying to extract dirty secrets from his unconscious (What letter? Your letter? Was that "a hair" or "affair"?), I gave up on sleep. I grabbed a pillow and moved to the living room, hoping the change in environment would help. To my relief, it was empty but still no sleep would come. I lay there, patting my postnasal drip with a ream of toilet paper and wallowing in a pool of self-pity. Then I looked over at the stack of ratty paperbacks on the windowsill. *A Portrait of the Artist as a Young Man. Slouching Towards Bethlehem. The Wind-Up Bird Chronicle. Last Exit to Brooklyn. Sons and Lovers. On the Road.* I was besieged by the sinking feeling that it had been over a year since I'd read a book in its entirety. I was a fraud.

I glanced at the clock on the cable box and reached for the phone. Never having called in sick to a job in my life, I had called in no less than four times in the past two months. Finally I was actually ill—while catalyzed by recreational substances and basic sleeplessness, my body still knew a low-grade fever when it felt one. But this was no time for the truth. It was Sunday night, and it's a well-known fact that calling in sick on a Sunday night is a fancy way of saying "three-day weekend." I settled on the infinitely dodgier but always effective alternative: a death in the family. I could even utilize my scratchy throat to create grief. Not wanting to jinx the living, I chose a beloved aunt who had died fifteen years earlier. For one thing, I knew she would approve. If I die tomorrow, I hope my living friends and family make such practical use of my demise. For another, it wouldn't technically be lying.

I was irrationally petrified that Ursula would be in the office and answer the phone in the middle of the night. The sound of her voice on her outgoing message made me nauseated. I cleared my throat. My aunt has passed away, I said, telling her that I would update her further when I knew about the family's plans for the coming week but she should count me out for tomorrow at the very least. There was a grain of guilt, but it was nothing compared to the tidal wave of relief that swept it away. I curled back up on the sofa and fell asleep as the sun came up.

I was awoken by the sound of Jimmy's phone ringing. I felt hung over and diseased-like. I heard Jimmy answer and put the voice on hold.

"It's your father."

"What?" I shot up, trying to put the puzzle together as fast as my neurons would allow. My lips were dry from breathing through my mouth all night, and they cracked as I mouthed, "How did he get your number?" Jimmy shrugged and I took the phone from him.

"Dad?"

"Are you all right?"

"What?"

"Are you all right?"

"I'm fine, what's going on?"

"Apparently I'm dead. That's what's going on."

"Is that how you got this number?"

I glanced at the coffee table with the lighters and Vietnamese take-out menus scattered on it. There was a square hand mirror with white residue caught in the edges, which I truly didn't remember being there the night before. Christ, wasn't it Monday? I imagined my mother's voice: *Who's doing drugs on a school night? Put the crack pipe away, kiddo. And stop using your flash cards to cut blow.* There was also an empty bowl with burned pot stuck to the inside. If inanimate objects could die, they'd look like that sad little bowl. I picked it up and sniffed it.

"I got this number by digging up an address book you left in your desk and calling everyone in it. Then I looked up their last names in the phone book and called their family's homes."

When had my father become a Mafia don?

"Where is your cell phone?"

"It died."

"There's a lot of that going around today."

"Wait, how many people did you call?"

My father had tracked down half my graduating class until he found someone who knew Jimmy's last name. It took him until noon to do this, so thorough was the humiliation carnage.

What happened was this: My scratchy throat worked *too* well, and the message I left came out garbled. Ursula gathered most of the staff into her office and played the message on speakerphone. Together they concluded that it was my father, yes, definitely my father, who had died. Lenore got wind of this and called my parents' home in White Plains to offer her condolences on my father's untimely demise. Which is when, back from the dead, he answered the phone.

"What's going on with you?" My father had shifted gears and was genuinely concerned. I was their baby girl and any irregular behavior was a sign that (a) I was in the first stages of cult initiation or (b) I'd been kidnapped and was in a basement somewhere doing Morse code through a vent.

Exhausted and feverish, I told him everything I had edited out for my sister. I relayed the details of what had happened not only that day, but as much as I could remember from the past year—leading up to my verbal patricide.

"Jesus." He sighed, paused, and hung up on me. Rightly so. The aunt in question was on his side of the family.

My next move was damage control. The friends who'd received a wake-up call from Dad could wait. I dialed Lenore's number and explained as much of the truth as I could. I told her that in my grief I must have slurred, and that my father was fine but my aunt was, in fact, dead. Could she do me a favor and tell Ursula this?

"Sure, honey," she said. "I'm so sorry. Though, it's funny . . . your father didn't seem to know about your aunt."

"This is a difficult time for him. Denial, you know?"

"It ain't just a river in Egypt," she sagely offered.

Ursula never called. A close (potentially parental) member of her assistant's family had almost definitely passed away and no phone call. I thought perhaps she knew my secret and wanted to spare me the embarrassment. But she was not in the business of sparing. Perhaps she knew and wanted to dangle said embarrassment over my head like a stinky cheese. Not that people generally hold stinky cheese over each other's heads, but if anyone would, it was her. I told myself that I could no longer work for a woman who wouldn't make a simple condolence call. But truthfully, I knew I had hit rock bottom after a very long fall, and that it was the length of the fall that did the most damage. She threw the manuscript, but I don't remember ducking.

Fake Dead Aunt Day was September 10, 2001, just over a year since my first day as Ursula's assistant. With Jimmy out of town on "business" and me afraid to face my own family, I spent the night at my friend Justine's parentally sponsored apartment in the West Village, where there was a fluffy fold-out couch, a working furnace, and a computer on which I typed my resignation letter. I spent more time on that letter than I had on the one to the post office. In the end it was four sentences and a "sincerely." Justine looked over my shoulder as I typed.

"What I don't understand is why you didn't quit after she threw the manuscript at your head. I would have been out of there so fast . . ."

"Sorry, what is it you do again?"

"I am the proud indentured servant of a brilliant art adviser."

"Who . . ."

". . . Who may or may not have purposely stapled my index finger to a manila folder."

"Thank you." I pressed Print.

The following morning I got on the subway headed uptown, letter in hand. Though resignation letters are not professionally required in the publishing world, mine was personally necessary. I was so afraid of speaking directly to Ursula, my plan was to hand her the piece of paper and stand there while she read it. I was envisioning this ceremony in my head when the subway train rattled, stopped, and moved again.

By the time I got off, both World Trade Center towers had been struck by planes. Our office being antiquated, everyone watched what was happening on an old black-and-white TV with rabbit ears, giving my 9/11 experience an instant and eerie historical quality. Eyes glossy, we cupped our hands over our mouths. Ursula took charge.

"Anyone who feels uncomfortable can go home," she announced.

I turned to leave.

"What's that?" Ursula stopped me. I still had the letter folded loosely in my hand. Oh, this old thing?

"Is that something I need to see?"

Clearly she thought it was some vital document whose chances of being lost or fucked up increased with every moment it stayed in my possession.

"It's not important. I was going to give it to you tomorrow. Or I can leave it on your chair. Or—"

She snapped her fingers, twice, quickly. I stepped forward and presented her with the paper. On the TV behind her, the Pentagon was on fire. Someone said, "I think we're at war," but I can't remember if it came from the long-eared box or one of the spellbound faces glued to it. Ursula gave me the last of her looks; this one said: "I can't believe that you'd do this to me with all that's going on in the world. Go find a coffee shop to work in, you waste of a girl."

For once I didn't care. I was as calm as I had been in months. The next day I interviewed for a new job, which I got. My future boss met me at a café, since the building that housed her office was in chaos or temporarily closed due to a bomb threat or something of that nature. Ambulances and fire trucks flew down the avenues. We held our noses, shook hands, and went inside.

People are always surprised by this. How could I have gone through with a job interview at such a time? We didn't know how dark things were or how much darker they were going to get. It was Wednesday morning, not "the day after 9/11." Devastated but ill-equipped to show it, we were all in a kind of limbo and we didn't know it yet. Like the flies that used to swarm around Jimmy's block, unaware that they lived on the lower east side of an island. That was us. It was the beginning of heartbreak, the beginning of paranoia, the beginning of revenge. But we had a few days of slow motion before it all set in. And for a big part of me, it was the end.

"Okay," Ursula said, folding my resignation sharply in half, "This is awfully formal. Do you have anything you'd like to add?"

I looked straight into her eyes. They were a vibrant green unflecked by anything but more vibrant green. This lent them a hypnotic authority. What must it be like to wake up every day with those eyes? Or to be the subject of their approval? Just as I found myself slipping into a view of the world from behind them, I pulled back and focused on the irises up front. They looked increasingly familiar and I realized that, in fact, I had gotten the cookie coloring right after all.

"Well," I said, fighting a smile, "I feel uncomfortable and I'm going to go home."

BRING-YOUR-MACHETE-TO-WORK DAY

In 1990, after our Apple IIE quit, our family purchased a Macintosh Classic. This was a good thing because the IIE was a constant source of confusion for me. For one thing, it took large flexible disks that were not even, despite all tactile evidence to the contrary, marketed as "floppy disks." The more current model—disks half their size and so hard you could eat off them—held the public title of "floppy." (Also neither of these options were, in fact, disc-shaped.) For another, the monitor would freeze or blink incessantly without telling you what was wrong, like a pet or a baby. I tried to fix it myself once and the Brightness knob shot out and hit me in the eye. As if these crimes weren't enough to make us love the Macintosh Classic by comparison, our new computer came with three free games. One of them was Oregon Trail. I have no idea what the other two were.

A game of moderately tough choices and rawhide, Oregon Trail wound its way through the late 1980s in a very un-'80s-like fashion: subtly. Unlike BurgerTime or Tetris, high-speed programs structured around multiple levels, Oregon Trail slowly moved toward a singular goal. It also had a distinct masturbatory quality. Here was something millions of preteens did, only you wouldn't find out until much later in life. Something one could do over and over again, with no diminishment of rewards. Apparently many children learned how to play it at school, which strikes me as just plain illegal.

For me, Oregon Trail was a private affair—something I engaged in after dinner when I was supposed to be doing homework. At the time I was going through a somewhat awkward phase, both the "somewhat" and the "awkward" being total understatements. I had a chin that jut out when I smiled, as if it were trying to escape from my face. And who could blame it? My eyes were too big for my head, my hair too big for my whole body, and my whole body too flat to be noticed by anyone but me. Sadly, as it is for many of us, my awkward phase found me years before I qualified for a driver's license or even the alarm code to the house. Homebound and date-free, I enjoyed an early teenagehood of drawing in journals, chatting with inanimate animals, prank-calling boys, and playing Oregon Trail. Oregon Trail, which provided me with the illusion I was actually going somewhere. Once the game began, I became completely enthralled, pausing only to listen for the pattern of stair squeaks that would indicate a parent was descending.

Oregon Trail was built on a completely unmodern premise.

This also distinguished it from its contemporaries—there were no robots, no time machines, no spacemen possible in a world where people ate unrefrigerated animal guts and washed their socks in a bucket. Originally designed by a couple of college students to teach kids about the odors and tribulations of pioneer life, the game starts in nineteenth-century Independence, Missouri, and heads toward the west coast. The screen itself—displaying a khaki stretch of land and a mountain range in the distance—never alters. It moves from left to right as your tiny wagon heads west, but there are no pop-ups requiring you to select a weapon, no shifts in perspective, no interiors. It's like watching some brilliant independent film where there are no cuts and no scene changes, only a wagon and a little thing called destiny. It's also like watching a lost ant crawl across the kitchen counter.

Though you never see their faces, you can choose your persona—a banker from Boston (likely a metaphor for Reagan), a farmer from Illinois (likely a metaphor for Carter), or a carpenter from Ohio (Jesus?). Each character comes complete with a skill set and a gun (just the one rifle—this was pre-Uzi). For a future vegetarian, I sure shot a lot of venison.

Unlike other games of the day, which had me leaping through traffic or called me "gumshoe," Oregon Trail left lots of room for creativity. It seemed ripe for the misuse. Like a precursor to the Sims, you were allowed to name your wagoneers and manipulate their destinies. It didn't take me long to employ my powers for evil. I would load up the wagon with people I loathed, like my math teacher. Then I would intentionally lose the game, starving her or fording a river with her when I knew she was weak. The program would attempt an intervention, informing me that I had enough buffalo carcass for one day. One more lifeless caribou would make the wagon too heavy, endangering the lives of those inside. Really now? Then how about three more? How about four? Nothing could stop this huntress of the diminutive plains. It was time to level the playing field between me and the woman who called my differential equations "nonsensical" in front of fifteen other teenagers. Eventually a message would pop up in the middle of the screen, framed in a neat box: MRS. ROSS HAS DIED OF DYSENTERY. This filled me with glee.

I actually began playing the game in 1990, but it still reminds me of the 1980s. For the sake of this Oregon Trail's influence, you have to ignore the date discrepancy. There's always a bit of cultural bleed between decades, and the segue from the '80s to the '90s is infamously fluid. Especially if you were still a child in the early '90s and the formative pop cultural markers of your life were four or five years down the road. It's the same reason Sunday morning movies can seem unquestionably from the '80s, but upon closer examination with a digital remote, were made in, like, 1992. Think of slouch socks, of Roxette, of Jennifer Connelly and Elizabeth Shue with full faces. You're thinking of the '90s. Much like the Macintosh Classic itself, the '90s took a while to power up. I find that anything culturally significant that happened before '93 I associate with the decade before it. In fact, Oregon Trail is one of a handful of signposts that middle school existed at all.

Which brings us to now. Here in the new millennium, there

are five versions of the game available, including an Amazon Trail and Africa Trail, but none has provided as much milk to the pop culture teat as the original. Now the wagoneers have realistic movements and facial features. Their adventures have become complicated. But at what cost? Would I be able to go on unceremonious killing sprees now as I did then? Perhaps now you can click a button and see the inside of the wagon, pioneer children napping through a shaky afternoon, dreaming under the dangling hides of eight rabbits and a moose. I know I will continue to wonder. I am too fond of my memories of Oregon Trail and not in the market to have them replaced. Also, I no longer own a machine that plays video games so my curiosity cannot be satisfied without a significant financial commitment. Apparently the game has changed for the better.

It wasn't long before Oregon Trail was criticized for its complete lack of Native Americans, African Americans, or three-dimensional Americans of any kind. The hunting came under a certain degree of scrutiny as well because apparently guns connote "violence." Then there was the game's blatant favoring of rich white males. The banker is by far the best choice for your pixelated proxy. He's in good health and comes with spare funds, which can be used to buy food in times of famine or the munchies.

Despite this orgy of damning evidence, I still think of Oregon Trail as a great leveler. If, for example, you were a twelve-year-old girl from Westchester with frizzy hair, a bite plate, and no control over your own life, suddenly you could drown whomever you pleased. Say you have shot four bison, eleven rabbits, and

Bambi's mom. Say your wagon weighs 9,783 pounds and this arduous journey has been most arduous. The banker's sick. The carpenter's sick. The butcher, the baker, the algebra-maker. Your fellow pioneers are hanging on by a spool of flax. Your whole life is in flux and all you have is this moment. Are you sure you want to forge the river? Yes. Yes, you are.

THE GOOD PEOPLE OF
THIS DIMENSION

In 1978, my mother painted an abstract picture of herself holding a red orb in her palm. Twenty-five years later, the painting fell on my head. I'd had it framed because I liked to pretend the orb was me, cradled in acrylic, though my mother insisted she painted it before she knew about me. It was hung above the bed (where I was sleeping in my first apartment on the Upper West Side) when it fell and gashed me awake. The painting was only the first to go. Two shoeboxes from the top of the closet plunged to their deaths and when I heard wineglasses shatter in the kitchen sink, I decided to do some investigating. I had a roommate at the time. I knocked on his door and opened it.

"You've always wanted to live in California," I said, leaning on the vibrating door frame. He was facedown, buried in the pillow. The pounding, which seemed to emanate from the very core of the earth, shimmied his alarm clock off the nightstand. I caught it in my hand.

"What the fuck?"

"I know."

He turned to face me, the rest of his body still heavy with sleep. It was 7:45 A.M. on a Sunday and the banging was so severe it made us wonder if firecrackers were being set off in the toilet.

"I don't think so," I said. "I don't remember leaving any fire-crackers in the toilet."

"Then, what the fuck?"

"Look at my head," I said, pointing to a bloody spot on my scalp.

We lived on the top floor of a walk-up and our apartment was the only one on our side of the hall. The building faced Columbus Avenue but we faced the old courtyard, filled with furnished gardens, terra-cotta pots, and the wind chimes that rich people had hung outside their brownstones. We were used to blue jays, not disturbance. In fact, prior to the *Jurassic Park*–style pound-ing, only one strange thing had ever happened before.

My roommate had just come home after dropping off his laundry across the street.

"What exactly is going on on the first floor?" he asked.

The first floor is really the second floor, which always struck me as very European until I moved in and had to climb an extra flight of stairs each day. Then it just struck me in general. He informed me that the front door of one of the apartments was completely off the hinges and leaning against the wall in the hallway. He said he'd peered into the apartment's living room, where he saw tiny supermarket bags stuffed round with trash and lined up in neat rows all over the floor. That, and a portal to another dimension. I said I had no idea what he was talking about. "And why does it always have to be another dimension? What's so bad about this one that a portal to Nepal or Claire Danes's TriBeCa loft wouldn't be enough?"

"Just go look," he said.

I went down the stairs to find the door closed, on its frame, with no sign of oddity beyond a bumper sticker beneath the peephole that read: "The weather is here. Wish you were great." I lugged myself back up the stairs.

"There's nothing there," I said.

"You're kidding, right? The door is blown off."

He could tell by my weariness of the topic that I was not kidding. When he returned from picking up his laundry a few hours later, he dropped the twenty-pound bag on our doormat.

"You"—exhale—"have"—inhale—"to"—exhale—"go see."

And so I put on shoes and went down and saw the shut door and then I waved to the shut door and marched back upstairs.

"It's not funny," I said.

A few days later, I left the apartment for work, clacking loudly down the stairs in a pair of heels so badly worn down they had transformed into tap shoes. I caught him. An old man who was more or less all ear was parallel parking the door into place with his bare hands, pivoting this giant slab of wood onto its hinges and locking it into place. I held tight to the railing above him and stayed very still. My neighbor Evan came up behind me.

"Good morning," he said. Evan paid six hundred dollars a month for his one bedroom.

I screamed. And then I pointed down to the old man with the door. "Do you know that guy takes his door on and off?"

He nodded. "Always has," he said. "He's OCD. That's how he gets into his apartment. He thinks that because he's on the first floor people have been touching his doorknob on the way up all day and so he takes the door off the hinges to open it."

"And puts it back on to shut it? You're kidding me."

"I'd make up something more believable than that if I was."

"Good point."

"He's also trying to dig a hole to China through the floor."

Three years passed before the painting fell off the wall. My roommate and I got used to "the lunatic on the first floor," and especially to the frenzied sound of the door scraping against the hallway tile when we came down the stairs. Sure, the occasional fashion magazine subscription card and bit of plastic bag would creep out from under the door and, sure, the only roaches I had ever seen were clearly on a foreign exchange program from his place, but we basically forgot about him. The way you forget about things in the city, despite daily reminders of their existence. My roommate called him "gross" on occasion and I agreed. Except on Sundays, when he called him "evil psycho spawn" and I agreed with that, too.

Because Sunday mornings were the digging hours. The door was shut so no one ever knew what really went on in that apartment and it's not like life provides you with a frame of reference for the sound of floorboards being ripped up with a pickax as one tries to tunnel oneself to Beijing. Once, in a fit of prematurely awakened rage, I stormed out of my room, threw on my winter coat and a pair of flip-flops, and pounded on the door on behalf of myself and all my fellow tenants. I was livid for all the obvious reasons and some of the not-so-obvious ones. Reasons that went something like: Some people have jobs and can't just stay home and tear up their bedroom floors because they feel like it. And when they're not at said jobs it's their God-given right to get drunk and sleep in on the weekends. I screamed, "Sir! Sir! Our windows are vibrating!" and the drilling came to a halt. Permanently. And there was peace. And it was good.

A few months later, the Italian restaurant we lived above posted a sign out front that read: CLOSED FOR RENOVATIONS. After several years of waving and nodding at the headwaiter while I smoked a cigarette on my stoop or dug in my purse to find my keys, I felt like he was as good as family.

"What's going on?" I asked him, nodding at the sign.

"We're building a patio out back for people to eat during the summertime."

Ah, I thought, the old edible patio.

"So we're going to start with the drilling," he added.

"When?"

"Not too early." He shoved his fists into his pockets. "Eh, maybe seven in the morning. Maybe seven thirty."

My roommate and I both knew that this was the beginning of the end. The construction workers, and they always came in the plural, brought with them buzz saws, motorized drills, and loud voices. The wind chimes would go the way of the dodo, the blue jays would seek out more muffled pastures. Even after the banging and the sawing had ceased, we knew there would be the clamor of an outdoor restaurant. This is New York, I reasoned with myself. This is the price you pay. But when they started doing actual construction on the weekends my thoughts turned to 311, the non-emergency services line. I went to reason with them. The sun had barely come up one Sunday and the restaurant door was open. I went straight through among the upside-down chairs and into the kitchen. I sang, "Helloooo . . . ?"

". . . And I know it's waking up more people than me if I can hear it on the fifth floor. What if you just started even an hour later?"

"Do you hear it on the weekdays?" he countered.

"Well, no, but that's the point, isn't it? I'm at work on the weekdays."

"Eh." He shook his head and gestured behind him. "And they're at work today."

Shortly after this exchange my roommate suggested we start throwing water balloons at the construction workers. Not really at them because, I know, I know, it's not their fault. But believe me, it's hard to look down and see a man with a seven-speed power drill plowing through a brick wall and tell yourself he's not responsible for the noise. We never actually hit them. The balloons exploded on some cinder blocks. "Assholes!" they'd scream up. "Bunch of assholes!" And this made us feel pretty great about ourselves.

On the Sunday after the painting fell on my head, they were at it again. My roommate was out of town and I was looking forward to having our tiny apartment to myself. I was developing a permaheadache. And then it began, a series of actions straight out of a Dr. Seuss book. *I did not put my flip-flops on, I did not, that would be wrong. Instead, I dialed 311 to tell the cops to come.* Our childish reaction of late was affecting my thought process. I told the operator my situation. She asked me if this was a commercial or residential complaint and I told her it was a mixed breed—commerce oppressing a residence. Since I didn't know the address of the restaurant and my weary ears had deduced that our building shared at least one wall, I gave the only one I knew: mine.

"It's the Italian restaurant," I explained, Judas that I am. "You can't miss it. It's the one that doesn't sell flowers or do your dry cleaning."

I thanked her profusely and went for a walk through the park to shake off my shame. I thought I'd had another few decades before my noise complaint years. All this postcollegiate getting up early and not wearing jeans every day was starting to wear on my temperament. I thought, what if this city makes me hate the world? I thought of that expression about leaving New York before it makes you hard.

When I got back to the apartment, the front door of the building was propped open, as it was wont to be in the humidity. There's a bump in the front hallway tile and when it's humid, the door swells and gets caught on it. But when I walked through it, I heard voices coming from the first floor. The large-eared man was standing with his head down, his door out of sight. Two cops with static voices coming from speakers on one hip and guns on the other were interrogating him. I froze against the wall and listened. I couldn't hear what they were saying. I crept across the street and under a bakery awning. It had started to rain. I called my roommate on his cell phone and left some message in which I apparently used the word "narc" in reference to myself about eighty times. Why weren't the cops at the restaurant? Then I remembered giving 311 our address and went back across the street. I held the already-propped-open door for the cops on the way out. The female one looked at me and made the crazy gesture around her temple.

"Some people are fucking lunatics," she said and walked away.

The idea that this woman, a New York City police officer who had seen the worst this world has to offer, thought *my* neighbor was especially odd made me feel at once relieved and awful. I decided I would knock on his door and apologize. I wasn't sure why or what I could do about it now, but this was the neighborly thing to do. This is what a good neighbor is, someone who recognizes the odd humanity of sharing the same plumbing and the same front door but never seeing each other. It is not, for example, defined by the willingness to call the cops on each other. I took a breath and rapped gently on the door. I didn't want him to think I was another cop trying to bust it down. Nothing happened. "Sir?" I said weakly. I felt ridiculous. Had I gone too far? For the first time I found myself sincerely wanting to interact with him. I knocked again, hard this time. As if it had been waiting for me, the door immediately fell backwards into the bags of trash and old clothes, huge but dead silent.

BASTARD OUT OF WESTCHESTER

If I ever have kids, this is what I'm going to do with them: I am going to give birth to them on foreign soil—preferably the soil of someplace like Oostende or Antwerp—destinations that have the allure of being obscure, freezing, and impossibly cultured. These are places in which people are casually trilingual and everyone knows how to make good coffee and gourmet dinners at home without having to shop for specific ingredients. Everyone has hip European sneakers that effortlessly look like the exact pair you've been searching for your whole life. Everything is sweetened with honey and even the generic-brand Q-tips are aesthetically packaged. People die from old age or crimes of passion or because they fall off glaciers. All the women are either thin, thin and happy, fat and happy, or thin and miserable in a glamorous way. Somehow none of their Italian heels get caught in the fifteenth-century cobblestone. Ever.

This is where I want to raise my children—until the age of, say, ten, when I'll cruelly rip them out of the stream where they're fly-fishing with their other lederhosened friends and move them to someplace like Lansdale, Pennsylvania. There, they can be not only the cool new kid, but also the Belgian kid. And none of that Toblerone-eating, *Tintin*-reading, tulip-growing crap. I want them to be obscurely, freezingly, impossibly Belgian. I want them to be fluent in Flemish and to pronounce "Antwerpen" with a hint of "vh" embedded in the "w."

Why go through all the trouble of giving a ten-year-old an existential heart attack by applying culture shocks like they were nipple clamps? Because, ten-year-olds of the world, you shouldn't believe what your teachers tell you about the beauty and special-ness and uniqueness of you. Or, believe it, little snowflake, but know it won't make a bit of difference until after puberty. It's Newton's lost law: anything that makes you unique later will get your chocolate milk stolen and your eye blackened as a kid. Won't it, Sebastian? Oh, yes, it will, my little Mandarin Chinese—learning, Poe-reciting, high-top-wearing friend. God bless you, wherever you are.

Uniqueness is wasted on youth. Like a fine wine or a solid flossing habit, you'll be grateful for it when you're older. Natu-rally, being born in a foreign country is not the only coolness savings bond out there, but it is an automatic vehicle into self-possession if there are no other cars on the road. Maybe you don't come from the mansion on the hill or the worst shack at the foot of it. Maybe you're not religious or a spelling bee prodigy. Maybe you're not the youngest of nine kids or the child of a B-list movie star. Oh, but imagine if you had a South African accent. At least foreign citizenship is something you can point to and say, "This is where I come from. This is who I am." I almost had it myself.

A sophomore in high school, I was successfully plodding through my suburban existence when my mother called me into the living room and told me we were moving to Sydney, Australia. For a year my father had been working at a division of his company in Sydney, communicating with us largely via fax. Then one day we had visas and passports and private schools picked out. I was nervous about leaving my life—change was one thing, but this much change smacked of the Witness Protection Program. I expressed concern about finishing high school at an institution paved in gingham, a place that didn't involve gum under the desks or drug paraphernalia in the halls. What kind of environment was that for a child?

"Everyone in Australia goes to private school," my father explained, a statistic that still makes little to no sense.

But soon Australian realtors were calling the house. I tried to talk to them for as long as they'd let me before I passed the phone over to my mother. They all sounded wonderfully like Olivia Newton-John. Had a pervert called up and faked an accent, I would have told them the truth—that my mother wasn't home—instead of employing the classic "She's in the shower." (Kids across the country have grown up accepting the idea that no one can harm your family if at least one of its adult members is in the shower. No one knows why.)

When my father first left, he had sent us the standard "Koala 'Bare'" T-shirts, with mooning cartoon bears, and liquid-filled pens with sliding Opera Houses. He sent us pictures of the Sydney harbor at sunset with fishing boats and yachts suckling the shoreline. We sent him pictures of our blind dog covered in snow.

It became clear that the prospect of moving to the bottom of the globe for good would require more extensive cultural immersion. Dad returned home for a week with Polaroids of his apartment overlooking the Harbour Bridge, with books by Australian authors, with strange sandwich spreads and rugby hats. I became fascinated with the idea of backward-running toilets but knew better than to determine the validity of this rumor by asking. Instead, I watched a science channel miniseries on the kangaroo and was fascinated to learn they drool on themselves to stay cool. I was anxious to see them bound through my backyard like deer.

On his second visit home, my father went to get into the car on the wrong side. He went on tangents about Shiraz. When he bought opal earrings for the women in our family, I knew we were being bribed into cultural submission. My parents, much to my general dismay, were never in the habit of bribery-as-parenting. When I opened that velvet box to see two iridescent dots staring back at me, I knew this was real: we were moving to Sydney for sure. I was sad at the prospect of leaving my friends and putting our beloved cats and our slightly less well-liked dog into quarantine for six months. Dulling the pain was the knowledge that my imminent foreign experience came at a time when I recognized that this was an investment in coolness—both an adventure and an excellent way to get into an Ivy League school back home.

I wanted to be Australian as soon as humanly possible. I went on a self-designed immersion program (me). I started watching tapes of post–Kylie Minogue/pre–Natalie Imbruglia *Neighbours*, an Australian soap opera popular in the UK for its mind-numbing, cliffhanger plots. These were about as intricate as one character's shoelaces coming untied and the question on the table being if the shoelaces would get tied in the next episode. If you've never had the good fortune to see Australian soap operas (*Home and Away*, another classic), let's just say they make American soap operas look like *Requiem for a Dream*. The unrated version.

This sugar-and-spice programming was in peculiar contrast to Australian *Vogue*, which boasted bare breasts both in the articles and the advertisements. Not to mention the Australian teen magazines. Thanks to a publication called *Girlfriend*, I know what "pashing" is. *Girlfriend* was incredibly informative. I found my new Australian best friends to be fun loving, occasionally nude, perpetually tan, devilishly into neon pink thongs, and frank about yeast infections. They were intimidatingly self-actualized. All their quizzes seem to come to a "girls rule, boys drool" conclusion, whereas all our quizzes lead to a "how to make him jealous" conclusion. I had a full-length mirror on my closet door that I used while practicing my accent. Once I drooled on myself and ran around in circles. Just to see if it worked.

And then one day it was over. My father loved the country and his love continues to this day, taking the form of random words assigned a *Crocodile Dundee* panache (See: "Girls! Someone get me a Phillips-head screwdriver from the *ga*-rahge!"). But just when I had mastered my drooling, my mother called me into the living room again and explained that Dad had decided to return to a career in the States. Ultimately there wasn't enough reason to pick up the whole family and fling us to the southern hemisphere. She held my hand. I felt the globe shift under my feet as the entire continent of Australia disappeared in a poof of smoke. I removed my opals from my ears and carried them up the stairs in a fist.

I have often wondered how I would have turned out had I finished my teenagehood down under. I think one can "turn out" up until age eighteen (I secretly hope there's *still* a remote chance I will "turn out" okay). Presumably I'd be less neurotic and a better surfer. Of course, Australia wasn't all good times and Foster's. What I perceived as the Australian spirit of frankness—the result of a criminal-, shark-, and plague-prone lineage that seemed to say "screw high tea, the jig is up"—extended to more serious topics as well. I remember very well one *Girlfriend* essay by a young woman who had been attacked on a beach. A bunch of drunken boys had lured her into a jeep and taken her to an abandoned lifeguard tower. The essay was detailed and illustrated with helpful tips for young girls (biting, urinating, wearing jeans) as well as what the girl herself would have done differently (not gotten into the jeep).

But at least it was something different and it felt real. Now what was I supposed to do? My Australian dreams had disappeared into the night like a baby in a dingo's jaw. I was stuck in White Plains, New York—the bastard child of Westchester County—and I was all the more determined to define myself in some other way. It's not that I so desperately wanted out of my teenage wasteland. In fact, the big problem was that there was nothing definite to escape. The walls of suburbia are as flexible as the grass blades that blanket it. The side effects of growing up "just outside of [insert major urban center here]" are many but practically intangible. This is logical given the fact that suburbia itself is a side effect and practically intangible. For instance, suburban kids are uniquely mean. They don't have the dangers of drive-by shootings or shark attacks to put things into perspective. The poor aren't considered genuinely impoverished and the wealthy aren't *rich* rich. Everything is muted. Other side effects include but are not limited to: inadvertent house arrest until the age of eighteen, the mall as ecosphere, jingling car keys as status symbol, an intimate knowledge of golf courses but a lack of global awareness.

I spent a lot of time waiting for things to happen to me, which is more or less as pathetic as it sounds. But not entirely my fault. There was a lot of suburbia in the movies during the '80s and '90s and in them teenage actions are always propelled along by some outside force—say, a giant pink dog-faced dragon takes you away on his back or the rich popular girl steals your boyfriend or you get tossed into a white van and kidnapped. Or you get lost in the Australian Outback with a band of unlikely but lively companions, one of whom is a potential love interest. Back in reality, you wait for the bus, you hang out in other people's basements, and you define "exciting" as chalking your license to get into bars that probably would have let you in anyway. Suburbia is too close to the country to have anything real to do and too close to the city to admit you have nothing real to do. Its purpose is to make it so you can identify with everything. We obviously grew up identifying with nothing.

Then one day you look in the rearview mirror of your existence and realize that you can see clear down the hill-less and curveless and bridgeless road of your life, straight to the maternity ward where you were born. And then you go to college. Where your bland past meekly follows, sluggishly scraping its feet on the floor.

It was in college that I came to understand that being born and raised in suburbia makes it difficult to lay claim to a specific type of childhood. I wasn't conscious as a small child that one day I would be required to attend parties and go on dates and identify myself as having been from a certain kind of home (rough or privileged), exposed to certain kinds of things (alcoholics or teenage suicide), into certain kinds of music (Nirvana or Nas). I was barely conscious of New Jersey, forget the notion that there were other elementary schools in California and private embassy schools in Bombay. Or, if I thought of them, I thought of them as being in an alternate universe, half frozen in time. I couldn't imagine what the kids there would be taught, what cartoons they were exposed to—only that everyone in Southern California had a view of the ocean and lockers big enough to stuff a nerd into. In my world the cool kids were rich, poor, smart, black, white. As long as you did drugs and were relatively attractive, you were okay. That was about as complicated as our one rule got, but it was the only one we had so we stuck to it.

My senior year of high school there was a fight in the boys' locker room and some kid got his ear Van Goghed with a pock-etknife. This wasn't particularly shocking at the time but in college it recycled itself into a story. It's not like I had been "knifed." Nor did I know anyone who was a good candidate for a knifing. I hadn't even been in the appropriate wing of the school to witness it. But I clung to the fact that I *could* have witnessed it as a way to make me feel as if I came from someplace I could point to, someplace where I could say, "This is where I come from. This is who I am."

Which brings us back to Belgium. A random country I chose with a little globe-spinning. Sure, birthing my child in Belgium is risky business. Being "the Belgium kid" could very well lead directly to a middle school existence peppered with Division 1 playground pummelings. I am equally aware that the word "Flemish" is hysterical to an eighth grader and that to hail from a country famous for its waffles, chocolate, and fried potato is to pray for a high metabolism. However, as I become less and less Australian with each passing year, I am increasingly willing to take this risk on behalf of my unborn child. Beyond a general case of suburban apathy, if anyone has a right to move her spawn to a major European port city and back, it's me. After all, I survived "Sloane."

Yes, my name is my cross and my copilot. "Sloane," a vowel-heavy name inscrutable to people of all nationalities, became my Sydney in place of an actual Sydney. Like a lunatic in the psych ward with only smocks and slippers for clothes, my name is the one definite thing I own. It is the one thing that stepped up to define me when my kangaroo dreams hopped lamely into oblivion. And, like all things unique, it came at a price:

1. Number of *Ferris Bueller's Day Off* jokes (included here are those specific to the dialogue when Ferris disguises himself as Sloane's father and picks her up from school): 3,567

2. Number of Sloane Square and/or Sloane Ranger jokes made by acutely observant British people: 457

3. Number of times I have been referred to as man: 890

4. Number of times I have almost been referred to as a man (see: "I thought you'd be a man."): 123

5. Number of times I have heard the phrase "I thought of you today" as a direct result of the "Sloan" plaque affixed to automated toilets in public restrooms: 94

6. Number of times I have heard the words, "Oh, like the cancer hospital": 851

7. Number of children determined to turn me into two syllables, by placing an "a" between the "s" and the "l": All of them

8. Names I am most commonly called by telemarketers: Simone, Slain, Siobhan, Flo, Stacey, Susan, Slater, Leanne, and Slow (Yes, my parents named me "Slow." That's because they hate me and made me sleep in the linen closet subsisting only on bath salts and Scope.)

9. Number of times I say I've never met another female Sloane and people become inexplicably defensive about their worldliness and say, "Well, *I've* met a Sloane.": 116

10. Number of times I have received an e-mail with my name spelled incorrectly in response to an e-mail originating from me and therefore making use of the correct spelling of my name and thus have passive-aggressively retaliated by leaving off the last letter of the sender's name in all future correspondence: 32. "Thanks for getting back to me, Rebecc."

I have had this conversation with other odd-named people—Xantheses and Joaquins—and there's something about having an especially different name that makes it difficult to imagine what you'd be like as a Jennifer. It was easier when I was little to dream of being a Jane or a Becky, because the possibilities are endless in general. Around the same time I was pretty geared up to be an astronaut. This was before I realized (a) I have no math skills and (b) I am afraid of heights, helmets, extreme speed, and antigravity chambers. All I knew was that the stars were cool and the moon was even cooler, as far as round, glowing things in the sky were concerned. With the cosmos as the limit, who was to say I couldn't be named Lauren? I even had some guidance, as my mother's, father's, and sister's names all start with D and my mother and sister even have the same initials. Could I have been a Danielle? Maybe. A Daphne? Perhaps. I wouldn't have objected to being a Daphne.

But now it's too late. Unlike imagining my alternate past as an Aussie or my unborn child's future as an Antwerper (Antwerpite? whatever; I'm not Belgian), changing my name is almost impossible to imagine. It's like imagining myself with a penis. Sure, I've seen them used but I'm not quite sure what I would do with one. Stare at it in the mirror as boys always vow to do with breasts if they could become women for a day? Occasionally there will be a character with my name on TV or in the movies. I find this incredibly distracting. I should hope this is not so much the fault of my vanity as it is the fault of my untrained hearing. I assume, when I hear the sound of my name, that it is referring to me. It's like watching commercials on the Spanish channel and comprehending nothing except the word "Coca-Cola."

My name itself has become a placeholder for the heritage and cultural grounding I never had. It's a frightening prospect— every single thing I have ever known or ever will know about myself hinges on six letters. Technically, my family is Russian and technically my name means "elephant" in Russian. This is a coincidence, but because I am neither obese nor big eared, I can share this fact with strangers and it comes off as flirty. Who is to say that "elephant" is not a term of endearment in Minsk? The French call their children little cauliflowers and nobody seems to have a problem with that.

The real story is that my mother got the name from a 1950s black-and-white movie called *Diamond Rock*. Apparently I am not a naturally curious person, as it took me twenty-seven years to make a real effort to get my hands on a copy of it. I was in White Plains for the weekend and came across one of my old issues of *Girlfriend* with a smiling freckled girl on the cover. Flipping through the magazine set off an especially strong craving for a hit of definition. Australia hadn't been mentioned in our house for some time and, starting with the magazine, my parents and I got to talking about old times, until we hit *Diamond Rock*. They assumed I had seen it. In the past I had put too much weight on the big (an entire continent) and the small (my single-syllable name) and perhaps this movie was Goldilocks's third bear—the "just right" version that could explain everything.

But that's not exactly what I got when I finally entered the world of *Diamond Rock*. Upon logging on to Amazon.com, several signs suggested this movie might not, in fact, be the key to my existential plight:

1. The movie is called *Diamond Head*, not *Diamond Rock*. This could very well be my fault. I'm not a very good listener.

2. It was made in 1963, not the 1950s, and in glorious color.

3. Even a semiofficial site such as imdb.com spells the character's name three different ways: Slone, Sloan, Sloane.

Things were not looking well on the self-discovery front but I remained convinced I was on to something. I slid in the DVD and pressed Play. *Diamond Head* is the ridiculously campy story of senatorial candidate "King" Howland (Charlton Heston), who has made his fortune through his very lucrative pineapple dynasty, and his sister, Sloan Howland (the beautiful blond Yvette Mimieux). Apparently the Howlands are fiftieth-generation Hawaiians despite the fact that they are as white as orchids. Sloan has been attending college on the mainland with her childhood friend and Hawaiian lover, Paul, and they have returned to the Howlands' private pineapple plantation to propose their plans to procreate. Sloan loves Paul. Although . . . when the movie opens she's wearing a glamorous dress in front of a mirror and he puts his arms around her and says, "Never take off this dress." I'm going to go ahead and spoil it by saying that she does indeed take off the dress. There are, in fact, at least six more costume changes, each one a slap in the face of true love.

The movie is full of Hestonesque bits of eloquence, like, "I love you. Damn it, I do." And: "I don't admire your sense but I do admire your guts. Even if I have to string 'em on a barbwire fence someday." It's a story of race and class, sex and tiki torches—a *Guess Who's Coming to the Luau*. Determined to marry Paul against her brother's wishes, Sloan says things like, "Someday all blood will be mixed and all races gone." Which is presented as sweetly enlightened and we are meant to ignore the vague ethnic-cleansing undertones. The gecko in the hut, of course, is that Paul has few good qualities and even fewer lines. He's presented as an ignorant tradesman whose love for our heroine is purely physical. After successfully completing the "five-year program" at college, he plans on living largely off Sloan's pineapple inheritance. But hey, whatever makes the racism more palatable. The good news is that Paul gets stabbed at a luau, resolving the whole sticky mess.

I ejected the DVD.

My mother tells me she named me after the character because she was fond of the name and Yvette Mimieux was "such a good, pretty little actress." I wanted specifics. I wanted that isolated bit of dialogue that made her think, "This is the name I'm going to stick my kid with for the duration of her natural life and beyond! Here is the philosophy I want her to fall back on in times of trouble. What would Sloan Howland do?" If I wasn't going to be named after a dead grandmother or a natural wonder or have my citizenship changed, I felt that she owed me this much.

"I liked the name, but I'm not sure it has anything to do with who you are."

"This is my point."

"You're acting like you were adopted and now you're searching for your adoptive parents."

"I guess I am, in a way."

"I don't know how to respond to that."

"Mother, I love you. Damn it, I do."

I have now had numerous viewings of *Diamond Head*, largely by myself but occasionally with friends whom I have subjected to the shamelessly self indulgent Paul is dead exercise. The disc menu pops up on the TV and I casually mention this is the movie I was named after, hoping that they will see what I don't. That they will come up with a good adjective for Sloan—"passionate," "intelligent," "steely." Anything besides just "blond." You would think I was watching the Zapruder film. The problem is, I can't be sure what I'm looking for. I'm not quite crazy enough to crumble into a spiral of nothingness if I find no meaning in a Charlton Heston movie. Is Yvette Mimieux me? Am I her? Are we both Sloan? Mother, is that you? Who knows. What would Sloan Howland do? She'd toss her hair and make a pineapple upside-down cake, that's what.

Turning to Mimieux herself looks like a fruitless tree as well. Not having the decency to be legitimately French (she was born in Los Angeles), Mimieux's star more or less faded after the 1960s. However, she got lucky on the cultural identification front: she was most certainly a movie star so we know she's got more going for her than an unusual name. And ten bucks says she's been to Sydney for a movie premiere. Alas, in the grand tradition of my hazy upbringing, I was not looking for anything particular from *Diamond Head*, but this is what I found:

Things about the Character of Sloan I Aspire To
1. She's a spiffy dancer.

2. She has an affinity for wide-brim hats and admirably lays off the pastels considering she was raised in a tourist destination.

3. She owns several ponies of the nonplastic variety.

4. One online review notes that *Diamond Head* is "not for people who do not like drama and certainly not for racist separatists." I like to think my life is like that.

Things I Do Not Aspire To
1. She has a moody side she refers to as "the spitting witch."

2. She eats pigs on spits.

3. She drives barefoot and runs in the sand (both terrible for the arches).

4. She makes several references to Paul making her "burn," almost like she's conjugating verbs. *I burn for him. He burns for me. We burn for each other.* One cannot help but suspect VD as a factor in their engagement. This comes up again when King defines a "hapahali" as "two people jumping around in the same skin." An image which, like the burning, is disgusting.

Neither Here nor There

1. After Paul's murder she goes to a bar in Maui and gets drunk on martinis and licks the spillover from the base before passing out on the floor.

This didn't leave me with much. Sometimes we don't know what we want until we don't get it. It's like meeting someone for the first time after hearing their voice on the phone—before you met them you'd have said you had no particular image of them; afterward, you inevitably say you imagined them looking different.

When my father came back from Sydney, it took me a few months to fully realize our family was never going to take the Qantas leap. I lost one of the opal earrings a few years later and a few years after that I broke the pen (the opera house only stays in one place now, which could actually mean I fixed the pen). I have decided to take my mother's advice and stop watching the same movie over and over. The funny thing is, I get the impression that neither she nor my father actually liked *Diamond Head* very much. It's hard to imagine that anyone outside of the pineapple industry does. But maybe they knew. They knew that we were a middle-class, semidysfunctional, felony-free, religiously inept clan, and they thought this name was something interesting they could give me. They randomly picked it, just the way I had done with the cold countries of the European Union. They wanted me to have something I could point to and say: This is where I'm from. This is who I am. Because a Sloane, by any other name, is actually an Yvette. With an *e*, of course.

THE BEAUTY OF STRANGERS

I know it seems like a late start, but I was twenty-two my first time. Like many women in New York, I lost it in the back of a cab. Unlike many, I got it back the next day. A man showed up at the address printed on my first business card and asked the receptionist if anyone had lost a wallet. These days, I barely remember to take business cards with me when I leave the house. Then, I was so thrilled by their shape and texture and significance, I'd carry no fewer than ten. I offered to pay the man, but he refused; he mumbled something about being in the neighborhood and took the elevator out of sight. After he left I discovered that he'd already paid himself seventeen dollars and a monthly Metro Card.

The important stuff, however—the wallet itself, the credit cards, the driver's license—was all there. Which might explain why, two years later, when I left my wallet in a cab again, I made none of the usual motions to erase myself. I canceled no accounts, changed no codes, and threw away no keys. My past thoughtlessness had gone virtually unpunished and thus with my often-inconvenient mix of faith and practicality, I decided to give it a week before I called Visa. A game of financial roulette. And on the seventh day, my wallet showed up in my mailbox. And it was good. Even the cash was still inside.

I tried to feign shock around my roommate, who left his belongings everywhere and always, never to see them again. Once his bike was stolen from our fifth-floor fire escape. I attempted to console him, telling him that if thieves had found a way to take it, they probably deserved it. Plus, they had left his helmet, which I found to be a kind gesture. When my wallet came back to me, he was in the apartment and thus I was appropriately grateful to and awestruck by the universe. But really: this kind of thing happens to me all the time.

It's not that I think I'm particularly lucky; I'm not. On some level, I'm conscious that it's a numbers game and the longer I live here, the more likely I am to court small disasters. For example, everyone I know who grew up a true New York City kid has been mugged at least twice. This is logical. But fortunately, the game doesn't manifest itself only in the negative. The other night, I thought I felt someone sneaking up on me and I knew my time had come. I just knew it. I felt a hand tug at my arm and turned, wide-eyed, to see a very tall woman. She said, "Sorry, but . . ." and then tucked the label on my collar back inside my shirt. I laughed, touching where the tag had been, and thanked her. It was then that I decided the city is looking out for me. As they say, "Now more than ever." And perhaps that's it—perhaps it's a post-post-post-9/11 humanity that's trickled down to everyday courtesies like not stealing other people's wallets. Perhaps it's simply that niceness has always been New York's best-kept secret, kept quiet to keep the tourists out, like how it really doesn't rain all that much in Seattle.

In all likelihood, what's happening is not as romantic as a shared front against the rest of the country, but rather a basic sympathy for our fellow urban dwellers. It's a "do unto others"—type selfishness. I probably wouldn't leap in front of a crosstown bus for anyone only because I wouldn't expect someone to do that for me. But I would expect them to tell me that my fly is undone and take a certain amount of pride in informing others of this myself. In the past five years alone, I have left my wallet in a cab an astonishing, nay, impressive, 6.7 times. (The .7 is for all the times I would have gone ID-less into a bar had someone not slid across the pleather backseat after me and said, "Forget something?"). With the exception of that first seventeen-dollar idiot's fee, my wallet gets returned to me fully intact every time. Every. Single. Time.

Am I jinxing this streak by exposing it here? Am I courting a trip to the Herald Square DMV? I did consider that. I also figured this would be the ultimate test of my theory that it's not me, not just my luck, but something more organic about the way the city works.

I was absentmindedly picking my nails and pondering all of this on the subway platform when a small Korean woman came out from behind the median map barrier and smacked my arm down. "Slun!" She shook her head and held my fingertips in a bunch. "No bite!" People turned to look. Apparently my mother had found a way to morph into this meticulous petite woman in a pink jumpsuit. No, I slowly realized, this was not my mother, but a different woman—one who had painted my nails three weeks prior at a local salon. She turned slowly away from me and sauntered down to the other end of the platform without looking back. After that, the question was no longer whether the city was looking out for me, but whether it was butting in. I like the barely there idea of a guardian angel. I could do without the babysitting police. When does neighborliness become meddling? It's got to rain in Seattle eventually.

With few exceptions, our actual neighbors who share our addresses are strangers as well. Naturally this does not prevent them from voicing their opinions about how we live. Recently, I came home to find a note pasted on my door with duct tape. Apparently I had been throwing my trash bags in the incorrect bucket outside my brownstone, thus leading to some bad bucket overflow. This deviant behavior had to stop. I felt the note was on the brusque side, but perhaps that was just the duct tape talking. Shaking it off, I plucked said note from my door and threw it out in the trash can under the sink. After about a minute of unrelated activity, I froze. I rushed back into my kitchen, flung open the cabinet, reread the Sharpie scrawl, and realized: this guy was going through my trash. How else could he know it was me? I now pulp my receipts, double knot my trash bags, and leave the occasional crumpled VD pamphlet in there for good measure. But the thing is, in his own inadvertently selfish way, I know he meant well. The man didn't want trash outside his house. And his casa is my casa, his island is my island.

In the end, it is rare that our random acts of kindness do not achieve their intended effect. It doesn't take much more than those magic words "hey, you've got toilet paper stuck to your shoe" to make me fall in love with this place again. Maybe I'm easy. Maybe it's all about inverted selfishness. That Cuticle Cop was well-intentioned, but because I would never do what she did, it pissed me off. I'm just not a good enough person to smack a stranger.

Thus, as I stood there waiting for my train, I felt my understanding and empathy for my fellow New Yorkers swell like a big glowing orb of Care Bears and butterfly kisses. I said the absentminded professor's prayer of gratitude for every glorious time a wallet-shaped envelope appeared in my mailbox. I smiled at people holding my same subway pole, and they smiled back. Because this is the beauty of strangers: we're all just doing our best to help each other out, motivated not by karma but by a natural instinct to aid the greater whole, one stray clothing tag at a time.

Except for the curmudgeonly guy on the corner of Thirteenth and Seventh who saw me smoking a cigarette and told me it would kill me. Asshole.

FUCK YOU, COLUMBUS

Every day in the not-too-distant lands of Westchester or Park Avenue penthouses (any category of "moving up"), people leave their homes to go to new homes, and their belongings go with them. They call movers and they go to brunch and they come back and all their stuff is in a new place. It's a simple process, really, a matter of physics and packing tape. But for those of us stuck on the ground, for whom penthouses come wrapped in plastic at the corner bodega, moving in Manhattan is a strange and fascinating hell. Anyone who has endeavored to transport themselves from point A to point B on this island has a story about "the worst moving experience ever." One person's CD collection goes missing; another tells of a magical moving truck that takes four hours to drive five blocks; yet another mistakenly spackles the dog. We've all heard it all. Well, almost all. The very nature of the gripe is to think that your story must be the worst. That said, I have a good feeling about the severity of mine.

Thursday, 2:00 P.M.: Being a New Yorker, I tend to instinctively value my belongings over my own life. I would never, say, liquor up my grandmother's antique crystal vase and send it by itself down the West Side Highway trying to hail a cab at 3:00 A.M. Thus, with plans to escort all my worldly possessions from my shared two-bedroom at Seventieth and Columbus to my current studio on Seventy-third and Columbus (I fear change), I call my new landlords and demand they install a new pad lock in addition to the basic one. I am set to pick up the keys to said lock on the following Tuesday. That's five days. I can wait five days.

Friday, 9:00 A.M.: After a week of stealing empty boxes and bubble wrap from the office, I start moving more fragile and valuable belongings (glass slippers, passports, vodka) on foot down five flights, up three blocks, and to my new place on Seventy-third. It's technically a studio but with fourteen-foot-high ceilings and windows in the bathroom, I like to think the heart of a one-bedroom beats beneath its floorboards.

Though my excitement about my own space is slightly tempered by what I am giving up for it. My roommate moves out Friday as well, abandoning me not only for a different home but for a different coast. This is a distressing experience for us both. Having had our fair share of certifiable or just plain malodorous roommates in college, we value each other as much for the relationship we have as for the unknown relationships we have narrowly escaped. We lived well together. I also had the bonus of living with someone with a healthy penchant for childish pranks. Into our newly adult lives there crept the occasional short-sheeting of my bed or setting of my alarm clock for an obscure time. And then hiding it. Who would keep me on my toes now? You can't exactly scare yourself out of the hiccups or glue your own toothbrush to the ceiling.

I want to sidestep any emotional good-byes. While my roommate—okay, ex-roommate—gets ready to leave for the airport, I spend most of the day keeping out of his way and scrubbing the mystery dirt out of my new pre-war (Civil? French? Indian?) apartment with every cleaning solution and Brillo pad I can find. I take fifteen or so "breaks" by walking over to the old place and carrying more things to the new. About thirty trips up and down the stairs later, I go out for the evening and return to the old apartment to sleep. I drift off, feeling overprepared and prematurely homesick for the coziness of a lower ceiling.

Saturday, 8:10 A.M.: I get up to prepare for the movers, who charge by the hour so I'm trying to do as much as I can by myself. I am wearing shorts, a tank top, and flip-flops. Why is this relevant, you might ask. Why is an early-morning outfit description ever relevant? For the first time in my three years of living at my old apartment, I lock myself out.

Saturday, 8:30 A.M.: After pounding on my neighbor Evan's door to no avail, it occurs to me that I should try to break in through the roof. I manage to unlock the roof door without the alarm sounding (a fact that would have bothered me tremendously if I had not been moving out that day) only to find that for the first time in his years at our apartment, my roommate has locked his window grate. But wait, *my* window has no grate. So I climb over the fire escape and, upon realizing that my toe barely touches the sill and this is not an action-adventure movie, climb straight back over and go downstairs.

Saturday, 9:00 A.M.: I approach a group of chain-smoking deliverymen hovering outside the Italian restaurant at street level. One of them lends me his cell phone. I call a locksmith. As I sit on my stoop and wait, leering at peppy weekend joggers, I think that maybe the locksmith will be my future husband. Maybe this will be the story we will tell our kids and speeches will be given at our wedding about hearts and the importance of having the key to them.

Saturday, 9:25 A.M.: He pulls up in an '82 Camry with his ponytail dangling out the window. The trunk is plastered with bumper stickers, the automotive equivalent of having a mullet. He says: So, you locked yourself out, huh? I say: Looks like it.

Saturday, 9:45 A.M.: It's a total of $280. Like most people who live here, I am prone to the constant suspicion that I'm being ripped off. But it's too early to process this. There's all this money, and then there's the shower and coffee it can open the door to. I hand him the cash. But wait, that's the money I had reserved for paying the movers. So I go to the ATM and take out as much as I can before the machine informs me with a friendly message: "You've reached your daily limit." I half expect a second window to appear with a helpful list of gambling and drug addiction hotlines.

Saturday, 10:00 A.M.–3:00 P.M.: Moving, cleaning, spackling, packing—a lot of "-ing." I am happy to be in my new place. I am even perversely thrilled by the dirt ground into the kitchen tile— it is my dirt that belongs to me and only me. Still, my calves are starting to throb. My friend James lives around the corner and he comes over to hang out, keep an eye on the movers for a few hours, and lend me money since everyone needs cash today and I can't access any more of mine. I'm exhausted and tired and sweaty and feel like I haven't slept in days.

Saturday, 5:40 P.M.: James leaves and part of me wants to grip his ankle as he does. I know he's going back to a settled apartment where no shelves have to be reconstructed, no sheets have to be unpacked, and no studs have to be found. I look around my new place and sigh at the clutter. I start to unpack and go to throw away a single box.

Saturday, 5:48 P.M.: I lock myself out again.

Saturday, 6:00 P.M.: I jiggle the lock to my new place, which will not move and which also sits about three feet above my doormat, which reads "Déjà Vu Déjà Vu," frontward and backward. This can't be happening. I jiggle some more. It's like the feeling of leaving your wallet in a taxi and realizing it's missing only once the cab has turned down the block, escorting your driver's license off into the ether. Your brain has yet to inform your hands that they can stop digging in your pockets now—it's over. Resigned to my fate, I knock on my new neighbor's door and borrow her cell phone. I call the landlord, who is somewhere in Connecticut. He informs me that the Super is on Ninety-sixth Street with a spare key that I can get if I go now.

Saturday, 6:30 P.M.: What do I really need now after two straight days of physical activity? A sprint! By God, yes, a sprint! So I book it up to Ninety-sixth and meet the Super. The Super will save me! Beautiful little man, I think I've never been so excited to see another human being in my life. I say: Are you the key

95

master? He says: What? I say: Nothing. He hands me the key and my heart sinks. It's actually a copy of the old key to the bottom lock. My landlord was wrong. This person does not have the key I need. He is, in fact, the devil disguised as a smiling Puerto Rican man. The disappointment fuels my run back to Seventy-third.

Saturday, 7:15 P.M.: This is not good. I sit on my stoop and breathe. My landlord won't be back from Connecticut until Tuesday. I can ring James's buzzer but I feel I've already asked enough of him. I would call a friend or a coworker or the ASPCA except that all my numbers and my phone for that matter are locked behind a big oak board. What's particularly annoying about locking yourself out or leaving a wallet somewhere or any mistake without prior escalation is that it could so easily have not happened. But it did. And twice in one day. And even if I could access my wallet, the ATM is determined to save me from myself and so I couldn't get cash until after midnight anyway.

Saturday, 7:45 P.M.: I do it. I call my parents collect from a pay phone. I think they think I'm in jail. I worry for a moment that this is their immediate assumption. Then again, something about the boxed pay phones in New York feels like TV prison anyway. This is around the time I unravel and start to cry. My lungs feel small. I tell them that I'm going to go back to my old building to read the same locksmith number off the same sticker and hope my old neighbors are home so I can borrow their cell phone.

Saturday, 8:15 P.M.: I tell the locksmith dispatcher that he should either give me a break or charge me double for being an idiot. Up to him. I laugh. He says he'll give me a twenty-dollar discount. I stop laughing. Meanwhile, my father drives into the city to bail me into my apartment: $260. He also brings with him a crowbar, a box of drill bits, and some wire hangers, which he uses in an attempt to crack the lock himself. This doesn't work, which surprises neither of us. It's getting late and my father goes home. I wait for the locksmith, sniffling and knowing all the lights are on.

Saturday, 9:30 P.M.: The locksmith pulls up. He is the same locksmith as the one from this morning. Hi again, he says. I tell him that he knows my life better than any of my friends or family because he is one of the few to have seen both my old place and my new one. He takes out his drill. I tell him that he has a very urban job, what with all the drunks and deviants and idiots in this city. I wonder aloud about all the strange people and places he sees. He peers into the lock and takes out a different drill. I tell him that I am not normally this irresponsible of a person. Or maybe I am but surely there are people more spastic than I. I guess this is lesson number one of living on one's own: make spare keys. I tell him I have very high ceilings and this will all be worth it. He changes the lock and fills out the receipt and points down with his pen. He says: That's a funny doormat.

ONE-NIGHT BOUNCE

The second I was old enough to know what sex was, I knew I wanted to have a one-night stand. To me, it seemed the most deviant, cool, subversive, and flat-out dirty thing there was. I wanted to do it immediately. Largely because I had no idea what it entailed. I figured a one-night stand happened when two people, one of whom was a woman, went to a man's apartment for martinis and stood on the bed the entire time, trying not to spill them. Sometimes they bounced on the bed until they hit their heads on the ceiling, and that's how the girl (a) passed out or (b) knew it was time to go home. This accounted for the sound of mattress springs creaking as well as any exhaustion the next morning. It was how hair became tousled. It also accounted for a very specific image I had, one of a woman in a silk teddy seen from behind. She's facing a window and it's probably nighttime. We zoom in on her hip, where she is resting her expensively manicured hand, with a pair of red sling-back stilettos hooked on her pinkie. Like a few notes of a song stuck in my head, that's all I got. I don't know who or where this woman is, only that between all the drinking and the bed bouncing and the near-concussion getting, the heels had come off. That explained why there was a lot of morning-after tiptoeing in movies and why no one ever had sex with their shoes on—it would puncture the mattress and twist the ankle.

It's remarkable the logic we'll build around a misapprehension. I used to think that to pass muster was to "pass mustard" and logic grew like a bonsai tree around my version to accommodate it. I figured the idiom had something to do with a yellow condiment being successfully tendered over a picnic table. Don't get me started on "intensive purposes." These things seem silly now, mostly because it's difficult to remember how we thought about the unknown before it became known. If people visit you at work and can't find their way to the right elevator bank, it seems strange. You find old flash cards with vocabulary words like "militia" and "loquacious" on them. You learn the globe, learn that Madagascar is nowhere near South America and never was. Suddenly the island is fixed in the bitch seat next to Africa, where it will stay from now on.

Such innocent confusions are like cognitive magic-eye posters. Most of the time it's impossible to go back to the jumbled mess once you've registered the picture. Sex is the exception. So natural and universal is a child's curiosity about sex and so long are we conscious of it before we do it, that our original impressions of it leave an indelible mark.

It's a point of fascination for adults that when it comes to sex, children are so adorably off base. At least Madagascar and South America are both landmasses; Lord knows what blowing on a penis has to do with a blow job. Or what jumping on a bed has to do with ejaculation. I never asked my mother where babies came from but I remember clearly the day she volunteered the information. My sister was taking a nap, my father was out back developing an elaborate pulley system for firewood using a laundry basket, and my mother called me to set the table for dinner. She sat me down in the kitchen and, under the classic caveat of "loving each other very, very much," explained that when a man and a woman hug tightly, the man plants a seed in the woman. The seed grows into a baby. Then she sent me to the pantry to get place mats.

As a direct result of this conversation, I wouldn't hug my father for two months.

As I grew older, sex became less clear but more fascinating. I knew I was being exposed to more of the song, but each note made my prior version sound less and less like the real thing. Never so bold as to volunteer my curiosity, I would receive sporadic information about sex, like encoded messages from the planet Libido. Once I tried to sneak into an NC-17 movie with my sister (NC-17, "not admitted without parent"—a fascinating warning since the idea of seeing a dirty movie with my parents was the most unappealing experience I could think of). We never made it past the popcorn stand. Dirty movies are like roller coasters: you have to be tall enough to ride them. Another time, in fifth grade art class, I was making something out of papier-mâché and googly eyes and a girl across the crafts table was amazed that I had not yet "done it."

"Who would I have 'done it' with?" I became defensive and tacked on the lie of, "Obviously I've made out with a boy before."

"I did it with my cousin last year."

That was the end of that conversation.

When I was fourteen, a camp counselor explained what "eating out" was and I vowed to never have it done to me. It seemed cannibalistic and unhygienic. I also remember that she claimed—in front of an entire cabin of girls—to have been "eaten out" by one of the maintenance men in a hot tub. Under hot water. Either something is amiss in my memory of this conversation or she found the most talented man on the planet and all hope is lost for the rest of us.

Then came a brief but vivid fascination with rape. Or what I thought rape was, before I understood that it didn't have a whole lot to do with sex. Likely, this is because I watched too much TV. On TV, when two people were about to have sex, they kissed and the lights faded and then they went into a room to do the horizontal tango. In the next scene, the woman came out of the bedroom in a terry cloth robe and the man had made a breakfast that included orange juice. Fresh squeezed. On occasion I saw a woman's breast or a naked man's back shifting on top of the woman like there was a skateboard between them. The only time I saw some actual nudity was in the after-school specials on sexual harassment, or in the extremely traumatic *The Accused*. In place of terry cloth robes and dimmer switches, which suggested sex was going to happen in a scene edited out between this one and the next—rape scenes by definition had to show some version of the actual act.

Gradually, I was gathering more and more information that might one day facilitate a one-night stand of my own. I knew that the underwear had to come off. I knew that if the woman wasn't turned on, sex could be pretty damn uncomfortable. I knew that alcohol didn't just make you happy. I knew that rape specifically was very bad and something to watch out for like broken glass and electrical outlets. But I also knew that before it strayed into a heinous caveman crime, sex was one of the ways in which people needed each other.

"Dolphins," my sister once informed me, "are the only other animals besides humans that have sex for fun."

The veracity of this was of no concern to me. I could only deal with one species' privates at a time and even that was proving difficult. With this deluge of images—between the maintenance men and the dolphins and Jodie Foster—it was only natural that my bouncing martini was getting lost. And the further my dream of innocence slipped, the tighter I tried to hold on to it.

I suppose it didn't help that around this time I was watching a shitload of *Twin Peaks*.

We were obsessed with the series as a family. Some families have Scrabble night; we had David Lynch night. My sister had a paperback copy of *Laura Palmer's Diary*. We unfolded the liner notes to the soundtrack (which showed thumbnail photos of every character) and stuck it on the side of the fridge. I kept a piece of fireplace wood as a pet until my mother reclaimed it in the middle of the night, citing the potential of ground dirt and bark on her freshly cleaned carpets. Recently, I became nostalgic for that profoundly piney northwest community and borrowed the first season of *Twin Peaks* on DVD from a coworker. I would have been about twelve when it aired, and watching it now, I was horrified at all the S&M references, sexual abuse, spousal abuse, midget abuse, owl abuse—the list went on. The corpse of a blond and blue and defiled Laura Palmer is wrapped in plastic and washed up on a riverbank in the first scene of the first episode.

I called my mother immediately to inform her that she was a bad parent.

"I can't believe you let us watch this. We ate dinner in front of this."

"Everyone watched *Twin Peaks*," was her response.

"So, if everyone jumped off the Brooklyn Bridge, would you do it, too?"

"Don't be silly," she laughed, "of course I would, honey. There'd be no one left on the planet. It would be a very lonely place."

"Mom, do you know what happened the night of Laura Palmer's death?"

"I'm sure you'll tell me."

"Before she got killed, some guys tied her up and screwed her while a parrot pecked bloody holes in her shoulder."

My mother was silent, contemplating this. She had a certain memory of *Twin Peaks* and parrot sex didn't factor into it.

"Huh." I could hear her shrug. "Well, I thought that show was a riot."

With enough *Twin Peaks* watching, I realized that bouncing on hotel beds was only "sexual" in teenybopper movies and short stories. I now saw one-night stands for what they were: a strange penis and a strange vagina getting to know each other fairly well, very quickly. But my original fascination with the one-night stand remained intact, even if the logistics had changed. And why not? Here was one last thing I could single-handily save from being muddied by adulthood. Here was one small innocent dream from my childhood brain. A dream there was no harm in believing (provided one kept their wits and prophylactics about them). It is so rare that we get to realize as adults what we imagined ourselves doing as children. Granted, this rule is generally applied to more wholesome activities like, say, intergalactic space travel or a career in the ballet. Nevertheless, I suspect this is why I hung on to my one-night stand dreams.

But by now, time was running out. Another decade and my invitation to the reckless sex-and-drug-abuse club would get revoked. Then people would be compelled to spit words like "floozy" into my face and they would have every right. It was suggested that perhaps I was not trying hard enough. That's probably true. It's not as if I had chronic bad breath or a neck goiter or other blatant physical obstacles to overcome. A couple of guy friends generously offered to help me remedy the situation, but their candidacy was null by virtue of the fact that they'd met me. And I wasn't about to walk into a crowded sports bar and scream, "I've got twenty minutes and one expired condom. Who's in?" Adventure within reason was key. Still, it seemed that it shouldn't be this hard. Who do you have to sleep with to get laid in this town?

My first legitimate attempt came during the spring of my freshman year of college. Armed with the knowledge that oral sex had nothing to do with talking, I met a prep school–issued member of the sailing team at a keg party. It was such a small college that the simple fact that we had never seen each other before was enough to get the conversation going. After eliminating all the telltale TV signs that he was a potential rapist, I went back to his dorm room. It was below freezing that night, and I had decided to wear taupe-colored stockings beneath my jeans and flannel socks over that. This is not a look that lends itself to a sexy undraping. It's also supermodel-proof, meaning that even a supermodel would look unappetizing in taupe-colored stockings and jeans. I tried to keep my new friend busy by kissing him while he began unzipping, but nothing gets past the human hand these days. He put a massive callused paw on my synthetically silky thigh, stopped, said "huh," and excused himself to the bathroom where he vomited (presumably from alcohol). Then we both crawled into bed and he passed out, drooling on my arm as it went numb from the weight of his head.

I felt relieved that he had gotten sick. Now the social scales of mortification were even. I watched him until six A.M. at which point I felt I had put in my time. I got up and wrote him a Post-it Note, apologizing for leaving. When I realized I had crammed in all I could on one yellow square, I grabbed another and filled that one with more witty remarks about seeing him around for some delectable cafeteria cuisine. Though one consisted of just my signature, in the end I filled six Post-it Notes, which I stuck on his computer monitor over a screen saver of rotating catamarans.

This was before *Swingers*. I would like to say that I crumpled them all up, making a delete key of my fist, and took them with me. I didn't. I was still blinded with embarrassment. In my one-night stand fantasies, there were never ever stockings. Or flannel socks for that matter. Garter belts, maybe, but not a pair of control-top stockings that left red indents around my belly button. Three months later, he graduated and I purchased my first pair of candy red high heels.

I realized that I had to be a little bolder if I was going to have a suitable one-night stand and that it wasn't going to be handed to me on a silver keg. My second attempt came during a semester I spent at Columbia University. Columbia seemed like a hotbed of people and options compared to my small and cloistered New England college. For one thing, it had grad schools. We didn't have grad schools. We didn't even have a football team. There were certain similarities, however, including the way the floors of the library became progressively less social as you worked your way up. The first floor was a meat market. The top was monkish. This architectural layering of academic intent seems widespread. But at Columbia, if I really wanted to get some studying done, I had to bust out of the building altogether and study in the law library.

This was a place where silence was platinum. One was glared at if one sneezed or shifted in one's seat. I could have come in naked with nothing but a grand piano strapped to my back and my only chance of eye contact would have been if I had leaned on the keys. The law library became my sanctuary, my home away from a home that included a roommate who hung full-color posters of Audrey Hepburn on her wall, recited Shakespeare, and regularly flopped down naked and soaking on my bed and said things like: "Tell me, is there anything more glorious or decadent than a shower in the middle of the day?"

I wasn't sure that there was. This was before I took up smoking, before I tried heavy drugs in any effective amount. This was a time before I bought myself flowers or clothing I didn't need. This was also a time before regular sex. Somewhere in my head a new image of the one-night stand had formed. It had all the good clean fun of bed bouncing but was now informed by the fact that I had seen a couple of penises and got the gist of what would go down on such an evening.

The Columbia law library looked like one of those very expensive stores that you can tell are expensive by the amount of space between the clothing on the racks. Just replace the shirts with people. It was also open late. I spotted a guy in one of the modern-looking chairs. I was burned out from studying but I didn't want to go home. God knows what show tune–heavy naked prancing was going on in my room. She also used to binge on Twix bars and pin the wrappers to her bulletin board. I packed up my things in case my encounter went poorly, marched over, and leaned in.

"Would you like to get out of here?"

"Why?" he asked with genuine confusion, and stared at me.

Unable to squeeze any more mileage out of my bravery, I said, "I'm sorry, I thought you were someone else," masking my shame by pretending I was a spy. The right answer to my question would have been given in code, like, "I would like to get out of here but it's raining on the plains." And then one of us would slip the other one some microfiche. I ran out of the library and never went back.

The following year it looked like my time had finally come. I was traveling around Europe with my friend Justine and I decided to give it another go. We boarded a train bound for Venice and thought it would be a good idea to sneak into one of the first-class cabins. It was an overnight train and in first class the seats slid down on both sides of the cabin, making the room a solid block of cushions. We found what we thought was an empty cabin, but opened the door to discover a nineteen-year-old Italian rap artist, sans entourage, or however you say "sans entourage" in Italian. He had a wide forehead and spiky black hair and two tongue rings. He wore a black button-down T-shirt, black jeans, and shock-white sneakers. He was also foreign and his very existence jibed nicely with my fantasies of raising my children abroad learning how to make good coffee. Justine wrote in her journal while I chatted it up with our companion. In perfect English, he apologized profusely for his poor English. He said he wished he spoke better but "that's the way it goes." I was trying to imagine how I would say "that's the way it goes" in Italian when a train cop knocked on the door with a couple of inexplicable German shepherds, checked our tickets, and booted my friend and me back to coach.

Hours upon hours later, unable to sleep from back pain, I remembered that the aisles of the first-class cabins were lined with a kind of nubby carpeting. I grabbed my book and lay on my back in the middle of the hall with my knees up. The lights flickered overhead as the train sped through the south of France. A hip-looking couple rolled cigarettes and smoked them with their arms out the window. People passing through stepped over me. Suddenly I saw the light in the rapper's car turn on. The couple in the hall was immersed in some debate in a language I couldn't understand. I knocked on the door and went in.

"Me again," I said, sliding the door shut behind me.

We talked, he handed me headphones, and I listened to some of his rap. And then he kissed me. Which is pretty narcissistic, kissing someone while they're listening to your music. The only thing that would have made it worse was if the song was about him kissing a girl on a train. Which it very well could have been.

The doors didn't have locks on them.

"We can do everything but," he said, and again, I marveled at his grasp of American phrases.

"Don't worry about me," I replied. And then, not wanting to look like a slut but still gunning for my one-night stand, I said, "We can do whatever comes naturally."

I felt like a guy.

"No, not naturally." He ran the metal tip of his tongue around the inside edge of his teeth. "I'm Catholic."

"Really? A Catholic rapper? I've never heard of such a thing."

"That's because you're American and all Americans do is violence."

And the Catholics are such pacifists? But I knew arguing

would only lead to more chatter so I accepted his Euro-slap and we did everything but. He threw out his back, I threw out my neck. It was romantic. I kept thinking: How is it that I got the one moral rapper on the planet? And: I wish the doors on this train locked. I had to keep dislodging my ankles, which persisted in slipping into the crack between the pulled-out seats. Afterward he gave me a mix tape, which I wound up leaving in a Danish hostel two weeks later. I returned to my coach car and woke up Justine.

"We're in Venice," I said.

"Already? What time is it?" She yawned and winced when she moved her neck.

"Already. It's seven in the morning."

"We better hurry up then." She stretched. "I hear it's sinking."

I never told her about what happened. When you travel for an extended time with someone, spending every moment together, knowing the location of each other's passports, sharing a bar of soap—sometimes you need a little something for yourself. Plus, I had failed. There was something tawdry and cheap about the fact that we did so much but I never slept with him. Actually, there was everything tawdry and cheap about it.

A few years ago, after I had long since given up the one-night stand ghost, I accompanied a girlfriend to an AA party. I had a cranberry juice and seltzer and I met James. Granted, he was vouched for, meaning that if he hacked me up to pieces and stored me in Ziploc bags, we had mutual friends and somehow that meant he would never get away with it. Still, he was new to

111

me. He suggested going to my apartment but I knew I had (a) a roommate and (b) my childhood blankey in plain sight. Plus, bringing him back to my bed made me feel like a prostitute whereas going to his place made me feel like a call girl. A nonsensical distinction that seemed important at the time. The next morning I woke to realize that not only had he put an extra blanket over me while I slept, and he'd ordered in breakfast, but he lived two apartment buildings down from me. In fact, our apartments faced out to the same courtyard and if we wanted to communicate through tin cans and string, we could have. Not only were we going to see each other again, the whole scenario stank of frequency. He was nice and clever and a generally pleasant human being who hadn't done a single reckless thing since the day he thought he could will objects to disappear and wrapped his brother's car around a tree.

I hadn't factored that into the equation, James being a good person. I slouched in his kitchen chair and sighed. He poured the orange juice and coffee. There was nothing to do but eat my home fries and ask him what he did for a living. And that was the beginning of a legitimately beautiful friendship. The other day we were in SoHo, shopping for sneakers for him.

"You've ruined me, you know?"

"How so?"

"You were supposed to be my one-night stand. Everyone should have one and now look what you've done. I'm going to have to go out into the world and sleep with someone else. You've turned me into a strumpet."

"Who said everyone should have a one-night stand?"

I stopped walking. Could he be right? Were all my attempts at achieving sexual normalcy for naught? It was as if he had casually mentioned the nonexistence of the tooth fairy to a kid who's all gums. For most of the forthcoming/drunk women I've ever encountered, one-night stands happen in between relationships, an attempt at recharging any romantic energy or just reassuring yourself that you're hot enough for strangers to want to touch their genitalia to yours. But I respected them. They were never filler for me. I treated them like a complete experience and what had they done but elude me? A one-night stand that plays hard to get. Fascinating.

"Maybe you're just not a one-night kind of girl," added James. "Don't look at me like that—in some cultures that's a compliment."

How was it possible that despite twenty-odd years of evidence to the contrary, they still struck me as sleek and glamorous and sometimes more worthwhile than a full-blown relationship? Then I remembered something I had seen when I started this ridiculous journey. I realized that if I could pan out from that picture I have—the one of the woman with the negligee and the red heels—I'd probably find her at a boyfriend's house. Maybe she's about to break up with him. Maybe he's about to tell her about the affair. Maybe this is her wedding night. Maybe this is what she wears to remove hair balls from the shower drain. As long as I stayed zoomed in, I'd never know. I bent down and took my shoes off. I wanted to walk barefoot in the dewy grass with them swinging in my hand. Except we weren't on grass. We were on Prince Street. I made it half a block before James stopped me.

"Enough," he said, "you're going to give yourself tetanus."

"Alright." I leaned on his shoulder with one hand while I put my shoes back on with the other. "But you should try it sometime. It's not as bad as you'd think."

SIGN LANGUAGE FOR INFIDELS

I don't remember exactly how long I was in that tiny, over-heated room. My presence there began on a road not so much paved with good intentions as sporadically littered with them. It was my first, and likely last, volunteer gig. Being blessed with one or two thoroughly selfless friends, I can say with a solid degree of authority that I am a selfish person. I spontaneously forget the names of more people than not, unless I want to make out with them. I will take the last square of toilet paper off the roll without thinking twice. I tip taxi drivers so poorly I'm amazed none of them have run over my foot while speeding off. Once I became so annoyed at a boyfriend's excessive use of my overpriced shea butter–based shampoo that I went out and bought him some Prell.

"You're so considerate," he said.

"Yes"—I clenched my teeth—"that's true."

I created something called the Good Intention Construction Co., a mental exercise meant to repair and beautify an otherwise broken and bland life. It's not a real company in the fact that it doesn't file taxes or order binder clips and it's entirely in my head. It's what pops up occasionally like an appointment on an electronic calendar when I become morally lethargic. Which is often. But I'm getting ahead of myself.

What happened was that just after graduation, I and some of the people I knew were contemplating our circumstances. Our circumstances being poorly paid jobs if we worked in the arts, two hours of sleep if we worked in money, and a newfound sense of intellectual inferiority if we worked in publishing. We were disillusioned by day and deglamorized by night. Our apartments, our love lives, the bar-slash-lounges we waited on line for. They all seemed smaller than we thought they should be. Eventually it hit a saturation point, all of us standing there in our nice shoes with our full stomachs and glossy lips—all the better to complain with, my dear. We needed some perspective, or I know I did. And so I closed my eyes and went to the Good Intention Construction Co. and saw that a ticker with a single phrase ran around the building's exterior: GO FORTH AND VOLUNTEER.

Being as selfish as I am, I wasn't sure this was the best prescription. I closed my eyes again, hoping if I shook my head, my brain would refresh itself like an Etch A Sketch or a Magic 8 Ball. Alas, the same message popped up. But where would I volunteer? I am not globally conscious by nature, and find people who publicly strive to make the world a better place to be moderately annoying. I resent it when they laud their worthwhile hobbies over me. I resent them opening mountain climbing supply stores in urban areas. I resent them brandishing clipboards and petitions on the sidewalk and the not-kicking of puppies. I never understood it. "Do unto others" (along with "a penny saved is a penny earned" and "fresh air will do you good") was a concept that had slid off me like water off an oil-slicked baby seal's back. Perhaps if I had grown up among the bears in rural Alaska, living off the fat of the land, or perhaps if my parents had been activists and professors at Berkeley, I would be a better person now. But I grew up in New York. The only real do-gooder message I absorbed was "don't keep jewelry you find in dressing rooms."

Of course I had *considered* volunteering. I think that once you know what something is, you have considered it. I'm far too solipsistic not to apply myself to every scenario that crosses my path. I remember the day I found out what an enema was, what spelunking was, that Asian women plucked their underarm hair, that the Golden Gate Bridge was an iconic springboard for suicides. I immediately considered jumping off it.

I was apprehensive about becoming a do-gooder. Real do-gooding is a religion. Do-gooders live in the same places, they believe in the same things, they eat the same things as long as they are labeled with freedom (wheat is among the more oppressed grains and it's important that we liberate it through abstinence . . . also lactose—Free the lactose! Free the gluten!), they shop at the same stores, and—most importantly—they believe there are things in this world far greater than themselves. Therefore, while there's nothing technically wrong with freeze-dried maple syrup and while I understand North Face tents serve a purpose if you work for *National Geographic*, I have become allergic to the presence of such things where I live. Yet, despite my fears that I would cross over into the light side, never to return, a little do-gooderism called "you should try something once" had stuck with me. Anyway, this was what united us, wasn't it? The universal desire to avoid being the asshole.

I took my volunteerism as seriously as someone like myself could. I knew my motivation was rooted in boredom; I wouldn't stick with it if it wasn't relatively easy. This narrowed the field considerably. Clearly orcas were out of the question, as were the disabled, women in need of JCPenney suits, the ozone layer, lead-paint prevention, historical landmarks, and anything involving a ladle. I thought about it long and hard. What cause did I deem most in need of my underqualified, halfhearted, likely-to-quit-in-a-month help? It hit me. I decided I could do the most good with a finite number of endangered South American butterflies at the Museum of Natural History's butterfly exhibit. If it was good enough for Nabokov, it was good enough for me.

So off I went, literally skipping to the museum, feeling special already as a security guard waived my admission fee and directed me to the volunteer office. I filled out a one-page application asking me my name, social security number, and address. I knew the answer to all of these questions! I was breezing through this sucker! When I got to "reason for wanting to work at the exhibit," I lifted my pen. I had a hunch that "because I don't want to shop for JCPenney pantsuits" was not the right answer.

I sat there in the volunteer office, unwrapping a butterscotch candy from a tray on the secretary's desk, squeaking back and forth in my orange plastic chair. Butterflies were a specialty of mine insofar as I owned an extensive collection of butterfly stickers as a child. Also, "butterfly" was the one word I know in sign language.

I looked down at my form.

Question: Why do you see yourself volunteering at the Butterfly Exhibit?

Two full-time employees came in to the office to get coffee. They had keys and large photo IDs hanging from their necks. They talked of strip poker and Paleolithic crustaceans.

Answer: I have always had a keen interest in biology.

This is not entirely untrue. I have always had a keen interest in biology. I've just never been very good at it. I remember dissecting frogs at camp and being so freaked out by their clear blood I had to take a break and have a cupcake. (It was always someone's birthday and there were always cupcakes.) Before returning to our picnic/operating table, I asked our counselor where the thirty adult dead frogs had come from. Without missing a beat, she looked me in the eye and said, "We found them that way. They were dead when we found them." I accepted this immediately, licked the icing off my fingers, and actually forgot about this conversation for some time. Only years later, when high-schoolers began dissecting fetal pigs a baker's dozen at a time, did it occur to me that just maybe that wasn't true.

The good news was that "biology" turned out to be the magic password for working at the Museum of Natural History, just the way "art history" would at the Met or "trust fund" at the MoMA.

Within twenty-four hours of walking through the door, I had my first adult volunteer job. On my application, I checked off the second-to-minimum time period possible.

I refused to get an ID badge. That was a whole separate form from a whole separate office and it pushed the boundaries of my commitment. In the few months I worked there, I was encouraged to fill out the ID paperwork several times, but every time the security guards stopped me at the back entrance to ask me where I was going all I had to say was "butterflies," show them my driver's license, and they'd let me in. Apparently it's only in the movies that people threaten to blow up museums and specifically the Museum of Natural History.

The museum opened the interactive butterfly exhibit in 1999. Since then it has become easily its most popular exhibit, as it is more zoolike than museumlike and provides a lively relief from the corridors of glass cases containing stuffed goats and model farm equipment. The museum itself has always been commutable from wherever I lived, by train as a child and on foot as an adult. Coming into the city for field trips, I knew about the great big whale and the dinosaurs in the lobby and the naively racist scenes of Native Americans shaking hands with English settlers on the street that would become Broadway. The exhibits, though still there, are surely products of a method of curation long since abandoned. I would speculate that the only reason they remain is that they have become a symbol of the museum itself. Its current curators must be grateful that giant swastika exhibit never quite took off.

In recent years, the huge museum banners hanging from the front entrance have reveled in the diminutive, boasting exhibitions on tree frogs and blood cells. Even the planetarium seems an attempt to capture the universe in an oversized golf ball. This, while a major celebrity narrates the story of the universe in gas and black holes, emphasizing how small we are. I now had to sit back and relax while a Hollywood star took me through a guided light show of my insignificance. I have to think the popularity of these exhibits is not disconnected from the butterflies, who have pioneered the smallness fascination at a museum that still has a tyrannosaurus skeleton in its lobby.

Picture the biggest bathroom you've ever seen. Now cut that in half and that's how big the butterfly exhibit is. It is less oppressive than a sauna but hotter than anything you'd find naturally in this hemisphere. A narrow twisting path winds its way through tall moss hills covered in green plants, orchids, and the occasional dish of orange slices on which the residents land and feast and discuss the events of the day. Perhaps a close encounter with a toddler. Or being mistaken for an *Asclepias syriaca*. Imagine! In theory, it should be a very Zen place and indeed the space is reminiscent of what some bored billionaire might have on the balcony instead of your average Park Avenue greenhouse. But on a crowded Saturday as many as twenty-five people—all emitting their allotted degrees of body heat—are funneled through the path by four volunteers. Some visitors are elderly. Many are children. Most have a lack of "indoor voice." All want to touch the butterflies.

There's a lot of pointing. A festival of pointing and at very close range to other people's eyes, given the width of the space. Also detracting from the exhibit's potential tranquillity is the display cabinet of pinned specimens along one wall. I found this disturbing from the start. You don't see a whole lot of stuffed polar bears in the polar bear exhibit at the zoo, for instance. And butterflies have phenomenal vision so it's not like they can't see the mass crucifixion in their midst. I was offended on behalf of the butterflies and thus pleased with my offense. Let the empathizing begin! This volunteering thing was working already. I am a good person, hear me give!

Once everyone is herded through, having caught glimpses of sulphurs and swallowtails, they exit into a mirrored chamber built to spot runaway butterflies. This chamber is so similar to a scene out of *Outbreak* that it led me to believe that the movie was more plausible than I'd previously thought and that some of these little guys could be poisonous. But I felt wimpy asking.

Eager to start my new life as someone who leads a fulfilling life, I arrived early my first day and Lindsey the Butterfly Volunteer Coordinator gave me the tour. I'm not sure what I expected of my fellow volunteers, maybe a few retired teachers and some private school kids looking to beef up their résumés for college. Lindsey was a Swarthmore grad with a BA in biology and a concentration in insects, currently in grad school for anthropology somewhere in the city. She wore a blue bandanna around her head of fine, long blond hair. Everything else about her was slightly mannish. She walked like she had a grasp on organic

122

chemistry and you didn't. Once I thought I saw her in Washington Square Park, out of the only element in which I had considered her. Upon closer examination I saw that not only was it a man, but a fairly unattractive one at that. I remember thinking how insulted she would be if she knew about the mix-up. The real Lindsey was kind and seemed genuinely happy to have me there despite the vast number of volunteer applicants who check "butterflies" as their chosen sector of the museum in which to volunteer.

"Do you live nearby?" she asked me. I nodded. Yes! I shouted inside. See how I have the makings of a punctual and educated volunteer!

"Well, then you might want to go home and change into sneakers and a darker shirt."

I was wearing a thin white shirt, jeans, and gold pointed flats. I opted to keep what I had on. I had been known to go out into a rainstorm rather than prance back up five flights to fetch an umbrella. Surely I could handle this. But within ten minutes in the exhibit, I was conducting a wet T-shirt contest for my armpits. Plus my feet hurt. From then on, Lindsey became my guru. She gave me a packet of information that included fun facts about butterflies. It contained words I hadn't thought of since sixth grade, like "phylum," proper Latin butterfly names, and every *Far Side* cartoon ever published on our flapping friends. That packet killed a lot of romance about butterflies I didn't know I'd had. Apparently they are the squirrels of the insect world. Gross little creatures in drag.

"You don't have to memorize it," she said, "but this should get you familiar with the questions people ask."

She was right. People are shockingly uncreative. A whole animal and everyone wanted to know the same things. Even the wisecracking dads all cracked wise in the same way (see: "How much butter do the flies have to eat?"). More mainstream questions that were impossible to answer honestly: how long do butterflies live? (one week, maybe two), how do they mate? (sitting, but they'll fuck 'n' fly if they have to), how many kinds are in the exhibit? (um, a bunch), how do they eat? (through a straw attached to their face).

The children were overwhelmingly morbid. Not a single adult asked me where butterflies go when they die, but this question was more popular than pixie sticks with the under-four-foot set. I cursed parents for not preparing their children. When I was five, my mother and sister sat me up on the kitchen counter and explained the facts of life: the Easter Bunny didn't exist, Elijah was God's invisible friend, with any luck Nana would die soon, and if I ever saw a unicorn, I should kill it or catch it for cash.

I turned out okay.

QUESTION: Where do the flutterbys go when they die?

ANSWER: Well, little girl, actually we spray them with alcohol, freeze them, and throw them away in a bin marked BIO-WASTE.

QUESTION: Don't the butterflies have a soul?

ANSWER: I'm guessing not, since they're so small. God knows where they'd keep it.

I wanted to go back in time and ask my camp counselor how she looked me in the eye and expertly lied to me about the frogs. I was, in a word, unfit. Unfit to lie to children. Unfit to tell them the truth. Who was I but a girl with a mission and a social security number? I had anticipated T-shirts or name tags or something courtesy of the museum. In fact, the only thing I had to wear to identify me as butterfly staff was a fist-sized blue button with a huge question mark on it. No "Ask me about our butterflies," no "Mind your own proboscis." Just a giant unsteady piece of punctuation that made me feel like I should be the one asking the questions.

I felt alternately superior and guilty asking people not to touch the butterflies. True, other people are scum and don't wash their hands after they go to the bathroom and even if they did, touching butterfly wings can kill the dear things. I, on the other hand, touched the butterflies all the time. I felt up my fair share of nymphalini all right. Simply because I was allowed to. I would pick up a giant slice of orange and let a blue morpho crawl off it and onto my finger. Morphos are about the size of a playing card. When their wings are folded up, they look like moldy chocolate moths. When they fly, however, the top of their wings are exposed, revealing the most solid electric blue I have ever seen. The death-obsessed midgets would come in the exhibit and "eww" at the specimen in my hand. I'd slowly tip my finger, causing the owl to spread its wings for balance and flash its blue like the inside of a trench coat. Then the children would "ooh" and "ahh" and I would feel that not only had I taught them a lesson about science but about life: You can't judge a book by its cover. Ducklings become swans. Blah, blah, blah.

Because I worked Saturdays, I even got to be there at the end of the week when a new shipment of butterflies would arrive in a tall black cage made of fine wire. It looked like it fell off the back of Darwin's *Beagle*. Before the museum opened, Lindsey would place the cage in the center of the exhibit and expertly remove the top, freeing the butterflies like they were lactose. It was a beautiful sight. Everything about volunteering was coming up orchids.

Except for the one particular winged thing that did me in. I situated myself near the front of the room because the Atlas moth lived in the back of the room. In that corner, measuring ten inches by ten inches, with other butterflies clearly visible through translucent patches in its fuzzy wings, the Atlas moth was a force to be cowered from. I would rather adopt a giant Peruvian hissing roach and parade it around Manhattan—holding it between my teeth—than lay eyes on an Atlas moth ever again. Its head looked like the head of a venomous snake, poised to strike at any moment. Atlas moths are, logically enough, referred to as "snake heads." Their backs are covered in a spindly kind of fuzz like a porcupine. In some countries, their cocoons are used as evening bags.

In the entire time I volunteered at the butterfly exhibit, I never once saw it move. Named for its worldly wingspan, which holds a replica of the earth-from-above in its pattern, the Atlas moth is the largest known moth on the planet. If the scientists discover a Paleolithic-descended underwater moth at the bottom of the ocean tomorrow, I don't care how freakish it looks: the Atlas moth can take it. It's nocturnal and, not being big on the whole flapping thing, it sticks to the side of the tree, wings out, feathered antennae up, creepiness high. I was petrified of the Atlas moth. I had nightmares about the Atlas moth.

I dreamed that I would come into the exhibit late at night. I had forgotten something. I would be the only one there but the heat would be on. A fluorescent tube of light would flicker above my head, revealing all the butterflies stuck to it—all except for the Atlas moth, who stayed fixed to the tree trunk, even in my unconscious. Just because I could, I'd lean my face in close to the moth.

"Boo."

And for the first time, the moth would move and it would . . . it would . . . eat me.

Actually, the nightmare was that it would land on my neck and refuse to be swatted away. But when I recounted my dream to Ruthy, my impressionable covolunteer, with the longest functional fingernails I've ever seen, I took it that crucial eaten-alive step further.

"That shit's nasty," she said.

"Well, let me tell you. It was."

"The Atlas moth can't eat you," Lindsey offered. "It has no mouth parts. It survives off larval fat until it gives birth and starves to death."

"Fuck, that's gross."

"Shhh," said Lindsey, gesturing toward a little boy in earshot.

127

"Oh, because 'larval fat' is so much less traumatizing than 'fuck.' "

Lindsey gave me a disapproving look and reached around her neck to tighten her bandanna.

"Ruthy," I whispered, "said the *S* word."

We were warned not to brush against the butterflies, but the five-year-olds were undeniably rubbing off on me.

Under normal circumstances, I might have been upset about being scolded by a peer. Especially a peer so well versed in a subject whose most basic building blocks I failed to grasp. That subject being social consciousness, not biology. It was a familiar situation. My volunteer job turned out to be not dissimilar to another joy-sucking position: retail clerk. Having spent my formative post-babysitting/preinternship years within ten miles of three different malls, I have held no less than five mall chick positions. The whole volunteer experience smacked of déjà vu—the tired feet, the (very) low pay, the loss of free time, the casual lying to customers. Except that instead of telling a spoiled anorexic girl that Bebe was out of stock in XXS black stretch pants, I was lying to children, and getting the Latin names of butterflies wrong.

I also recognized from my retail days the small but distinct thrill I got from working somewhere "prestigious." It was the perfect snooty conversation piece. Sure, I got those retail jobs for the money. My allowance disappeared on my twelfth birthday, along with my lunch being made for me, my bed being made for me, and "hugs." But if you had offered me a high-paying job at Aldo Shoes versus a low-paying one at Louis Vuitton, I would have taken the job selling overpriced baguette bags any day. In mall culture, there is a hierarchy and a camaraderie between the high-end stores.

At one point I worked at Oilily, a Dutch women and children's clothing company that sold two-hundred-dollar cow-print jackets for newborns. Black was banned and company clothing encouraged even if you had to borrow it for the day. I found myself wearing fluorescent orange stretch pants (mine, of course) and a hand-knit baggy sweater with swirls on it (theirs). This, I thought, surely this is better than working at Aldo. I tried to avoid leaving the store during lunch for fear of being shot by a hunter. But at least I had my dignity.

My best friend worked down the hall at Lacoste and would periodically send me envelopes of alligator stickers through the intermall mail with a note: "You've been lacosted!" My other best friend (they're like cars when you're a teenager; most suburban families have at least two in case one breaks down) worked upstairs folding shirts at the Gap—but we liked him anyway and he let us abuse his discount. It was a time when we were proud of ourselves constantly and for nothing. Our first jobs! And look how we had mastered how to abuse them! Eventually, the best friend who worked at the Gap moved to Florida only to work for a different Gap and the one who worked at Lacoste was arrested for the kind of shoplifting where instead of stealing from the shelves, you steal from the register.

Yet, even without these dramas, our bubble-like mall existence would have come to an end. You had to do more—go to college, pick a major, get a boyfriend, a job, an interesting scar, a dream house, an educated position on the death penalty. Suddenly you had more mail, more keys, more passwords, more toiletries. And all for less praise. People are less quick to applaud as you grow older. Life starts out with everyone clapping when you take a poo and goes downhill from there. If you stop and think about it, it's a miracle that we get out of bed every day and brush our teeth and remember to buy toothpaste. We all deserve to be congratulated but sadly that would mean there's no one left to do the congratulating.

I have a very distinct memory of watching Martina Navratilova pat herself on the back after losing in the women's final of the U.S. Open and not being properly acknowledged during the trophy ceremony. The crowd chuckled. That image pops into my head more than I care to admit in my adult life. I knew I wanted the same thing Martina had wanted when I knocked on the museum's volunteer office door. I didn't need a grand slam title, although that would be nice, I just wanted a pat on the back from a hand that was not my own. After all, if a soup kitchen is set up in a forest and no news crews are around to see it because they all saw *The Blair Witch Project* and they'll be damned if they're setting one foot into the woods for some stinkin' homeless people, does it count? Somehow I don't think so.

But there was no one to congratulate me. Thus, my fervor for my volunteer stint began to dwindle. The combination of forgetfulness and self-centeredness was lethal to my budding charity career. The first time I forgot to show up I had gone to the movies with my mother. Just as the lights dimmed, I remembered I was meant to be at the museum. My seat was a springy one and only too happy to help me bolt upright.

"What time is it?"

"Quarter past eleven."

"That is not good."

"Well, you're not going to leave now, are you? The previews have started."

She had a point. But it was not the point of a responsible adult. Always a stickler for "doing the right thing" when I was growing up, my mother surprised me now. I decided to interpret her blasé attitude as a sign that she saw me as an adult, responsible for my own decisions if not actually capable of making them. To rush out to the exhibit would have been to ruin my mother's movie date with her grown-up child. It occurs to me now that perhaps if I was ladling minestrone by the quart somewhere above 125th Street, she would not have been so serene. At the time, her reasoning meshed perfectly with my desire to see *How to Lose a Guy in 10 Days* and the subsequent free eggs Florentine. I squeaked back in my chair.

What annoyed me was not that I had missed out on volunteering. It was not that I had let the butterflies down and now some fifth grade Future Psychopath of America was on a wing-ripping spree. What annoyed me was that I so often attempted to weasel out of things on purpose, it killed me to do it by accident. It seemed like a waste of whatever detailed lie I was going to have to come up with. I would have had twenty minutes left on my shift when the movie let out so I called Lindsey, knowing I would get her voice mail. I told her the truth, that I had completely forgotten, and then I made a joke about the minimal obligation. We were two weeks in, which meant I was unreliable only 50 percent of the time! I am pretty sure that's not how commitments work, but it sounded good. I told her I looked forward to coming in the following week.

The following week came and I showed up. But the week following that I forgot again. The dreamlike revelations—that panicked feeling that I was meant to be elsewhere and immediately—startled me like night terrors. If remembering you had to be somewhere else could take the shape of a person, it would be a mugger in an alley. There I was walking along the street, on my way to pick up my dry-cleaning, and a man in a black mask would pop out of nowhere with a gun made of guilt.

Another time I slept in and leaving the house as soon as possible meant I would still be an hour late. So I played dumb and cited a schedule confusion.

Much to my mystification, they let me stay. One could argue that because I volunteered the minimum amount of time possible, I should at least show up. Thankfully, they seemed to view my sporadic appearances as I did—so rare, they were difficult to depend on and therefore difficult to be disappointed by. Most likely, it's problematic to fire a volunteer, even a half-assed one. It would be like breaking up with someone because they're too nice. Carnations again? You bastard.

After a while I became irritated by their unwillingness to fire me. Had I not behaved poorly enough? Was absenteeism so slim a crime? Apparently. I walked into the exhibit with an expression that attempted to convey the major personal problems that had prohibited me from showing up the past two or five times. When the first child asked me about butterfly death, it was like the final pin into the fragile crisp wing of a specimen: volunteering wasn't for me. Perhaps I would have been better off at a less cushy institution, like a homeless shelter where death is the last thing that needs to be explained to children.

QUESTION: What happens to butterflies when they die?

ANSWER: I honestly don't know. They stop flying, for one thing.

QUESTION: Don't they get angel wings?

ANSWER: Yes, that sounds about right.

The kid shrugged and meandered down the path. I checked my watch. I had five minutes left on my shift and took a nostalgic look around the place, lamenting that I could probably never come back as a civilian.

Like the retail positions I had held before it, the imagined glamour of the volunteer job had drawn me in, but wasn't enough to keep me there. I was familiar with this ruining process so I knew what to expect. At the end of the day, I rushed for the door, an anxious expression applied to my face. I tripped backwards attempting to maneuver around a pair of Japanese tourists. I caught myself, but not before my bare elbow brushed against the Atlas moth.

A shudder began at my funny bone and spread to the hairs on my neck. I shut my eyes. Maybe it was not the Atlas moth but some . . . some very fuzzy tree bark? Within seconds, a series of forbidden images plowed through my mind: this was like the opening of Pandora's box, the eating of God's apple, the crossing of the streams in *Ghostbusters*. I glanced furtively behind me to see that I had shifted the sleeping moth ever so slightly. Now it hung off center, the way a painting does when you bump into it in a narrow hallway.

Tainted by an overpowering grossness, I don't remember walking so much as flying through the doors and past the security guard standing in the mirrored *Outbreak* chamber. I walked at ramming speed through the back entrance of the museum, up the delivery driveway, and straight to my apartment, where I went up the stairs, skipping two or three at a time. I slammed the front door behind me and headed for the bathroom sink. I needed to rid myself of Atlas cooties. I grabbed a towel with one hand and excessively pumped hand soap with the other. It was unfair: I had already decided to put the kibosh on my days as a volunteer. I was on my way out, leaving in a manner that finally suited my ostensible job title, and I resented that the butterfly gods felt the need to let the Atlas moth hit me on the way out.

And it was at that moment, when I glanced up at my reflection in the mirror, that I saw I was not alone.

I gasped. One of the smaller butterflies was stuck to my shirt like a lapel pin. It was neon yellow with brown-tipped wings that looked like two pieces of charred paper when it moved. The fact that I had run through the room of mirrors without checking myself for stowaways I understood. The fact that the wind created by my speed walking had inadvertently pinned the little beast to my chest, I understood. It was the fact that it had chosen me of all people to land on that boggled the mind. After everything I had done to neglect its kind, this thing still chose to follow me home.

I pushed my finger slightly underneath its head until it crawled up my wrist and flew onto the shower curtain, which was covered with a pattern of brightly colored butterflies. This made it difficult to keep track of the three-dimensional one's whereabouts. I shut the bathroom door. I had to think. Instead of thinking I remembered that I had left the bathroom window open. I grabbed my cell phone and rushed back into the bathroom and shut the window. The butterfly had not moved. I didn't even know its proper name.

It was almost five P.M. I sat on the toilet and called the ASPCA. I was directed to a phone system that asked me to report the nature of the abuse. There's a whole button reserved to report barking. I looked at the butterfly. The butterfly looked back at me. It all seemed too official. The ASPCA would probably give me a case number longer than the wingspan of the victim. Also, I would have been implicating myself in a lepido-napping. My selflessness had its limits.

I hung up. It seemed more and more like something out of a children's book—the butterfly that followed the little girl all the way home to her fifth-floor walk-up. How above-the-law children's books are. Hansel and Gretel (littering, breaking and entering), Rumpelstiltskin (forced labor), Snow White (conspiracy to commit murder), Rapunzel (breach of contract). "What am I going to do with you?" I said aloud. It occurred to me that I could get into real-life trouble for this. Perhaps if I had been a worthy volunteer I would be granted some leniency, but I had already proven myself a delinquent. How far off was "thief"? As it turned out, shoplifting—the extreme sport of the American mall—also had something in common with my volunteerism. Then again, is it theft if the item flies up out of the store, lands on your shoulder, and follows you home? If only Hermès scarves and Fendi handbags did the same thing, women would clamor to work in retail.

I thought about reopening the window and setting the butterfly free. This seemed like the romantic thing to do. It was without doubt the fairy-tale thing to do. But then I figured it might starve (negligence) out on the mean streets of the city. How many orange groves were there in Central Park? Or it might get eaten alive (involuntary manslaughter). Or be poisonous to the pigeon it was eaten alive by, thus causing an inexplicable mass epidemic of rabid pigeons (very, very bad). I thought about keeping it. But it would never survive in my apartment. I don't own a Darwin cage thingy. Its bright poison-colored wings flapped open and shut. I could kill it myself. Let it crawl into the toilet and press down on the flusher. I hit a squirrel once while learning to drive. It wasn't pleasant, but I lived through it. I could kill again if I had to.

This decision wasn't for me to make. I opened the bathroom door just enough to let myself out into the kitchen. Mops, check. Brooms, check. Where was Nabokov's giant butterfly net when you needed it? I walked into my roommate's empty room and picked up his bike helmet. I turned it over a few times, tossed it gently in my hands, and put it back. I paced in the kitchen. Finally, equipped with a plastic colander and a wooden chopping block, I captured the butterfly. It had come voluntarily this far so I wasn't sure why I felt the need to keep it confined now. I looked through the holes of the strainer. The butterfly was suspended from the top of the dome like a bat.

It stayed that way the entire walk back to the museum, a trip I made with the steady steps of someone with dynamite strapped to her torso. It was getting dark. A mother and her little girl passed me on the sidewalk. The little girl craned her neck at the colander and I could just feel a question about to be asked. Christ, I thought, is this what it's like to own a golden retriever puppy and take it for a walk? Or to be eight months pregnant and take yourself for a walk? Why do people always want to put their hands on vulnerability? I sped up.

"I'm so sorry," I said to the butterfly, who didn't move. "I can't even remember if you have ears."

I climbed the front steps of the museum, balancing my goods as if they were a dessert in a metal dome, but the doors were stuck shut when I pushed on them. The overhead lights were out. The T. Rex was getting his beauty sleep. So down the stairs I went, knocking on the service entrance door. For some reason, no one was at the desk by the door. In the distance, a security guard passed by a row of computers. I put the butterfly down gently on the pavement and rapped on the glass. I couldn't tell if he saw me or not but pretty soon he would be out of my sight, under a marble archway. As I had no laminated museum ID to press against the glass, I was running out of options. I made the sign for "butterfly" in sign language to the security guard. If he couldn't hear me, I had no reason to believe he could see me, but in my desperation I hooked my thumbs together and wiggled the rest of my fingers. He passed under the archway and up the stairs.

Despondent, I ambled across the street to the entrance to the park. I moved the colander slowly across the cutting board until a space opened up, flipped it dome side down, and let the butter-fly go. I expected it to flee happily into the trees. Pigeon epidem-ics be damned. Go forth and spread your incurable diseases, friend. Instead, tentative and traumatized, it hung out on my side of the wall, eventually landing on a homeless person sleeping on a nearby bench and covered in quilts. I stood there watching them for five, ten, fifteen minutes. I remember thinking that now would be the time to give money to the homeless. I was over-whelmed with the poetry of the moment. Not a soul would be around to pat me on the back for committing this kind act and for once I was okay with that.

One of the few things Lindsey had taught me about butter-flies came back to me. Many of the poisonous ones aren't born poisonous. It's not yet pumping through their cells when they escape from their cocoons. But they feed on milkweed as soon as they have the equipment to do it and that's where the toxins come from. So there's a moment at birth when they could choose something else. They could choose to be better, to be gentler, to be of no harm. Of course, butterflies have been feeding on milk-weed since before we existed. A biological defense mechanism, it's not in the cards for them to feed off anything else. If it was, it would only make them more palatable to vicious jungle birds that would eat them for breakfast. It's a lose-lose situation.

I stealthily approached, not wanting to wake the man beneath the quilt or scare off the flapping thing that seemed so comfort-able perched on his shoulder. At the end of the month, I would receive an invitation to the end-of-season annual butterfly volunteers' party. I never RSVP'd and I never heard from the museum again.

The butterfly winked at me gingerly, opening its wings for a moment and then leisurely letting them shut. I opened my wallet. All I had was a twenty.

I looked at the butterfly.

I looked through my pockets.

I looked at the homeless man.

I looked through my purse for change.

I looked at the twenty again. Then I tucked the money beneath the quilt before I could change my mind, folded my wallet, and walked away.

YOU ON A STICK

There are two kinds of people in this world: those who know where their high school yearbook is and those who do not. I do not. Never did I expect to find myself, almost ten years after the prom, back in my hometown, at the base of a cul-de-sac, high heels sinking into someone's front lawn like it was quicksand. A victim of sanctioned déjà vu, I was smiling for the camera, flanked on both sides by women wearing bad dresses and flowers to match them. Once again our limousine came with plenty of upside-down glasses but no alcohol. Except this time the plan was to make a quick pit stop at the altar before we hit the dance floor.

There's a natural Darwinism of the brain that forces most people to let go of high school. We need our paltry three percent storage space for more contemporary information like the location of car keys. This is why childhood phone numbers sneak away like socks in the dryer. It's why the names of once beloved teachers get whittled down to the vibe of a single letter. (See: "It starts with an *L. L* something . . .") The order of life events gets fuzzy, as if it were not your own life but the life of some historical figure. Did Charles VIII get syphilis before or after he invaded Italy? Was I using tampons before or after I learned to tie a cherry stem with my tongue? I can never remember. And if any set of memories has a bull's-eye on its back, it's those from the four years leading up to the senior prom. We lose or, worse, we manipulate our memories of this time. It is my belief that people who speak of high school with a sugary fondness are bluffing away early-onset Alzheimer's.

So imagine my surprise when I received a phone call from a long-lost high school friend asking me to be in her wedding. High school was the last time I had a formal group of female friends that exceeded, say, three. We shared a lunch table, a yearbook page, and a near-debilitating fear of STDs. This particular friend and I were quite close when we were five feet tall, playing in each other's backyards and writing letters from our respective summer camps. But as we grew up, we also grew apart. As if there was this half-visible Cheshire cat ushering us through our social lives, she went one way and I went the other. By senior year I had forgotten where her locker was. We had exchanged nary a birthday card in the decade since.

There was a steady electronic vibration against my desk. I watched my cell phone seizure with the unregistered display of a 617 area code. Boston? I thought, Who the hell is calling me from Boston?

"Hi, Sloane! It's Francine," she chirped.

I responded with the same degree of skepticism I use for people with clipboards who employ familiarity as a means to get me to sign petitions.

"Sloane, it's Francine."

My mental Rolodex began to spin. Bingo. Francine Davis, Class of '96, Latin Club President, Video Yearbook, pot yes, liquor no. Wait a minute. High school? Was I, unbeknownst to myself, one of those girls that peaked in high school and stayed friends 4evR as the backs of our yearbooks decreed we would? Sixteen-year-old me would have been flattered by this notion of female solidarity. Twenty-six-year-old me was freaked out.

"Hey there." I cleared my throat. "How are you?"

"I'm engaged!"

Incidentally, this is an unacceptable answer to that question.

"Oh, that's great. Wow, it's been so—"

"And," she continued, "I want you to be in my wedding."

I was stunned. I pulled the phone away and looked quizzically at the hole-punched speaker. Aside from the blood obligation to be my sister's maid of honor, it had never occurred to me that I would get asked to be in anyone's wedding. I thought we had reached an understanding, the institution of marriage and I. Weddings are like the triathlon of female friendship: the Shower, the Bachlorette Party, and the Main Event. It's the Iron Woman and most people never make it through. They fall off their bikes or choke on ocean water. I figured if I valued my life, I'd stay away from weddings and they'd stay away from me.

They were easy enough to fend off. At few postprom points

have I had a large circle of girlfriends. I have certainly sat at brunches, looked around at the delicate wreath of glossed faces before me, and thought: *Finally. I did it!* But like a chemistry experiment, it seems stable for a moment just before it disintegrates. I could never keep invisible girlfriends, never mind the solid kind.

Moreover, I wasn't raised with weddings. Being the youngest of a small and relatively unsocial family, I was twenty-three when I attended my first wedding. Funerals? Funerals I could do. Picture a graph charting the luck of the entire Kennedy family. Now make them all smokers. That was us. But weddings? I knew nothing about weddings. I never had the childhood experience of being a flower girl. I never saw the word "marriage" and thought: Big party. Free cake. Sips of champagne! I didn't know enough to dream in fondant.

Then one day I woke up in my midtwenties and boom: I was attending one every three months. It was an epidemic and I was invited. Though never ever "with guest." While I understand financial constraints, when you begin to realize that at any given wedding, there is a better likelihood of you being "with child" than "with guest," something is very wrong. Hand to God, I had a dream the night before one particularly isolating ceremony that I was a duck-billed platypus, begging Noah to let me on the ark, but he refused because my other duck-billed platypus was riding the baggage claim carousel at the foot of the dock.

Beholden to no one, being a single guest also made me ripe for labor. I understand the need for programs but why must I be the one to fold them into paper cranes? Is this not why God created immediate family or, at the very least, interns? And if you're going to rent 250 folding chairs, why not get the kind that don't splinter in your girlfriends' hands when said girlfriends stand in the rain propping them into rows?

ME (picking wood shrapnel out of my thumb): Say, where's Lucy? I thought she was going to help.

BRIDE: Oh, she's with her boyfriend.

Truth be told, it was the more intangible tasks I found straining. I can stuff save-the-dates with the best of them, but it's the conversations one has midstuff that I found challenging. It suddenly seemed that a lot of those drunken nights and private jokes about bad dates were no longer an end but a means—fodder for the rehearsal dinner speech. Watch closely: If a woman has one eye out for a potential husband, chances are she's got the other out for potential bridesmaids. And yes, this does turn her into a cross-eyed freak.

Once, at a coworker's birthday party, a woman I had met twice announced her engagement.

"Congratulations." I lifted my plastic cup of wine.

"Save the date," she responded, squeezing my hand.

I didn't know the name of her fiancé. I didn't know where she lived. I knew her last name sounded like "crevice," but I could never remember it. I was definitely getting a *C* vibe. Yet she felt she knew me enough to invite me to one of the most sacred events of her life. And that was just the beginning.

It wasn't long before oversized envelopes started appearing in the mail every two months. Like a tidal wave stronger than the vows themselves, they could not be stopped. Gold calligraphy came swirling under my door while I slept. It crept into my closet, taking stock of my strappy sandals and pastel pashminas. It curled and swirled and wrapped its vowels around my wallet. I could click through the Williams-Sonoma registry blindfolded. The phrase "it's the thought that counts" had become hyperliteral as I spent more and more time calculating my bridal expenditures. Yet for all the financial burden, I had grown accustomed to my rank as Random Female Guest #7. I thought if I could just get through my twenties and thirties flying under the radar, if I could just stuff the occasional envelope and get passed over for the actual bridal parties . . .

And then Francine called me to be part of her wedding party. A wedding that was to go down in the middle of July. Oh, the humidity. Out of all the girlfriendships in all the world, what made her call out like a foghorn for mine?

"Isn't it great?!" I could hear her grinning through the phone. "Boris and I. Married!"

"Yes!" I involuntarily squealed. And it was. For her and for Boris, whom I had never met.

The subplot of modern marriage assumes that a wedding is the crown jewel of any best friendship, a time when otherwise rational women are legally permitted to misplace their minds, and treat their friends like heel-skin-shaving employees. This is something we tolerate of our closest pals, but I had barely spoken to this woman in a decade. If I got married tomorrow, chances are it wouldn't occur to me to invite Francine. It's a wedding, not an episode of *This Is Your Life*. I thought: What's wrong with her? I thought: Where is her big group of girl-friends?

I thought: Hypocrite.

So I agreed because, barring exorbitant plane fare or typhus, you can't not agree. Not only is it a social slap in the face and a personal kick in the feelings, it also puts a silent price tag on the friendship, no matter how faded that friendship is. If the average bridesmaid's dress costs $250 and the average bridesmaid's shoes cost $125, and you refuse to participate, that's like saying you wouldn't pay $375 to maintain that friendship. It's like saying if deranged pirate terrorists kidnapped the bride and demanded $375 and a few hours of your time in exchange for her life, you'd hand them the musket yourself. Sure, Francine and I had drifted apart and the last time we hung out we were wearing Z. Cavariccis and intentionally shattered heart pendants. Mine said "be fri," hers said "st ends." Sure, I couldn't remember her middle name or her natural hair color, but what kind of bitch lets someone get kidnapped by deranged pirate terrorists?

I had no choice but to respond not only with a "yes," but with a "yes, I'd be honored." On one tacit condition. There was an unspoken understanding that I would be standing up there with her as a one-time favor. In an effort to mask her apparent lack of sociability as an adult, that evening the role of "old friend" would be played by yours truly. Like the best man's polyester-blend tux, I was a rental.

In order to get married these days, God isn't witness enough. You have to have someone present who helped find your retainer after a sleepover. Although some overlap is permitted, the women you see each week are almost never the same set of women lined up behind you at the altar. Your current friends are wild cards and while they may be invited, they are not to be tortured with envelope licking. Marriage is about the permanence of one's future and it can't proceed without a well-earned past of trick-or-treating and bloody ten-speed accidents. As Francine's "something old," I felt sorry for her but would never say anything of the kind and, in return, she wouldn't make me wear baby pink.

Even after being part of the wedding, the most vivid thing I can remember about Francine dates back to the seventh grade. My father drove five or six of us to a dance at our middle school, which was in a semiabandoned part of White Plains, close to a highway and between some houses with no front yards. A few years back, they shut the school down and combined the middle grades—sixth through eighth—into a single middle school on a castle-like compound closer to the Scarsdale border. I have no idea what became of the old building I had my formative slam book years in. Like any red-blooded American kid, I like to imagine my middle school as a ruined catacomb of a crack den with boarded-up windows and junkies sleeping beneath the blackboard where I got every algebra equation of my life wrong. In my case, there's a good chance I'm right.

To the dance we all wore skirts with polka dots, each one with various-sized dots. I also wore an exceedingly hip combination of a see-through top with a bouquet of solid roses in the middle and earrings that made it appear as if a gold-plated dolphin was diving through my lobe.

Francine was the last to be picked up and my father, as usual, was embarrassingly early. He had his hand on the steering wheel for a third honk when Francine came out of the house—a vision in duct tape and sling-back jelly shoes. She had ripped up the pages of *Seventeen* and *YM* and duct-taped glossy models into a collage and, somehow, applied it to her body in a stiff dress shape. Twirling on her porch like a pinwheel spoke, she was straight out of the Betty Friedan paper doll book. On some small level we must have realized the irony of taking this unspoken body ideal, literally ripping it into pieces, and wearing it on your underdeveloped breasts as fashion. Parsons students have been given honors degrees for less. At the time, we only knew she looked cooler than Jem and her Holograms and Barbie and her Rockers combined.

She accessorized with a plastic charm necklace that included a snow globe with a dolphin in it (dolphins were a favored animal of the time), a working abacus, and a battery-operated toilet that made a flushing sound when you opened it. I was so proud to be her friend. She was brave and creative and that night we walked into the gymnasium in a girlish clump. We sat in the corner and played MASH (Mansion, Apartment, Shelter, House). When we were ready, we got up and danced like idiots.

"You down with OPP?!" I screamed along to Naughty by Nature, bounding my awkward and bony twelve-year-old body off the shellacked floor.

"Yeah, you know me!" Francine shouted back.

And I did. And that was seventh grade.

"I think it would be great if you all lost at least five pounds before the wedding."

With her marriage vows just under a year away, Francine was calling on a weekly basis to confirm details and broach paranoias so distant it was hard to make them out on the horizon. "That way," she continued, "you can all eat whatever you want during the rehearsal dinner and still feel normal the next day."

"Normal?" I pinned the phone to my shoulder with my chin and pinched a layer of flesh away from my stomach.

"But what if people are skinny already?"

"Oh, God, of *course* you're all skinny already. It's entirely up to you if you want to fast the day before. Or the week before if you do a juice fast. It's just, well, you know how Helen can get."

No, I didn't know how Helen could get because I didn't know Helen. I had never met Helen, one of the three other bridesmaids. A stunning expansion on my role as make-believe best friend was the requirement that I also make-believe in a whole web of friends. This would not be the first or the last time reference was made to someone's personality or husband or cup size. And I was expected to have intimate knowledge of every bit of it, as if the details had been IVed into me in my sleep.

"I'm sorry, Helen?"

"Helen Nolan. Lisping gymnast."

"Oh, right. Helen."

"But she's taken speech lessons since high school and she sounds fantastic. That is to say, she sounds normal. I think she just gets caught up on the *s*'s."

"Helen went to high school with us?"

"She was a few years older. Not that Helen has anything to do with it, but I just want my wedding to be as smooth and normal as possible. I want everyone to have an awesome time."

"Awesome."

"I want everything to be easy for you guys. You're my friends, not my slaves, right?"

I couldn't be sure if this was rhetorical or an actual question, in which case I would need a moment. I was quickly learning that one couldn't go wrong with giggling as a response to anything she said.

Example:

FRANCINE: I've just now learned that baby pandas everywhere—as well as some species of seal—are nearly extinct as a result of a rare strain of human influenza that has been traced to a coughing fit I once had at the Bronx Zoo.

ME: Tee-hee-hee.

"Seriously, though, no bridezillas here." She laughed too hard, sighed at the end of it, and slyly removed her own name from the crazy person hat.

Dietary constrictions were not the only logistical considerations brought up in the calls before the wedding. It was during these calls I came to understand that the "maid" in "bridesmaid" no longer stood for "maiden"—it instead bore the stench of Pine-Sol and dirty dishes. The presence of "maid" combined with the absence of "guest" is lethal. "Friends not slaves" indeed! These calls consisted of various instructions regarding transport to the wedding, table arrangements, the suggestion we wax our legs ("Of course, I would never *make* you ladies do anything"), and my bridesmaid dress. Here's a tip for brides everywhere: tell us what to wear and be done with it. A huge mistake is to tell your women that "any dress will do" as long as it's turtleneck and taupe. Do you think we can't see through this faux democracy? It's a bridetatorship. It's fine; it's what we signed up for. A wedding is about assumptions—the assumption of forever and the assumption of expenses. Understand that we will be purchasing a dress we would not normally purchase and there's nothing you can do to change that. Just wrap us in peach crinoline sacks and call it a day.

This capacity for an executive decision was lost on Francine, replaced by a growing expertise in passive-aggression.

FRANCINE: I want everyone to pick out their own baby pink plaid.

ME: Baby what?

HER: Baby pink. Baby pink *plaid*.

ME: Will Boris be wearing a kilt?

HER: We're not Scottish.

ME: You're not Scottish.

HER: And I'm having Stacy do everyone's makeup.

ME: Stacy?

HER: You know Stacy! And there's a fabric store in Yonkers. I'll give you the directions. They sell all these different plaids in raw silk!

ME (with a flaming cartoon dollar sign above my head): Raw silk?

HER: Don't worry, it's not too heavy. Don't want you gals sweating your makeup off!

ME: How much makeup are we talking about here?

HER: And you'll all have a choice this way! And—you know me—I'm making you these *gorgeous* hot pink headbands as bridesmaid's gifts!

ME: Sounds great. How many kinds of pink plaid are there?

HER: I just want everyone to feel beautiful.

ME: Why? It's your wedding. I think you should make us wear burlap.

HER: They don't stock burlap.

The second and far more troublesome kind of call—even worse than the laxative-inducing diatribes on water weight—was the "quick, let's bond so it makes sense you're in my wedding" call. With the out-of-town area code betraying her, I'd treat myself by letting her calls go straight to voice mail. But it was plain rude to ignore them all. I didn't bargain on daily reminders of having to be in Francine's wedding when I had said "of course," but there was no turning back now. During this second type of phone call, I learned that she was in business school, had just purchased an antique armoire, and was still allergic to bananas.

Eventually she began to pick up on my distaste for these conversations. One day we were mid–wedding chat when she said, the way people do, "It's important to have you by my side." (When else do we say this to each other in life? Descending into the basement in a horror movie? Whilst storming beaches? Elbow deep in cashmere at a sample sale?) "I consider you to be one of my best friends."

"Well, I get that. And I want to be by your side, too."

This was a lie, but one she had been fishing for all day. I was below the surface looking up at the hook and thought: We're gonna be here all day unless I bite.

"I'm so happy we're talking like this—I don't want you to stand up there as this random girl I went to high school with."

I was shocked and embarrassed. Exactly! I thought. Why someone who I remembered as priding herself so on marching to the beat of her own mandolin would insist on creating bridesmaids out of thin air was beyond me. Had a society of chick flicks and sororities made her do this? Had the cultural pressures been too difficult to silence? Had they become like the dog next door, barking orders at her? *I don't want you to stand up there as this random girl.* All I know is that if I reach forty and don't have a child, I'm not going to go out and kidnap one. Though not illegal in most states, asking me to be a bridesmaid struck me as a similar act. With this last comment, she had regurgitated the thing I thought most shameful about this entire charade, holding it up in front of my eyes so I could get a good look before she repeatedly smacked me over the head with it.

"And you know what they say," she sang in her Latin club alumnus voice, "*dulce et decorum est pro patria mori.*"

"What does that mean?"

"It is sweet and glorious to die for one's country."

"Of course it does."

"You mean of course it *is*."

I couldn't make sense of it and, stupidly, it never occurred to me to try. I stopped picking up the phone and started responding to e-mails only. I went through the motions, drove to Yonkers, bought the plaid fabric, had the fabric tailored to her specifications, bought the shoes, had the shoes dyed. For the shower, I chose a large registered-for hamper from Pottery Barn tall enough to lean on as I struggled to keep "dirty laundry" references out of the card. In the end it read: "Congratulations on your upcoming nuptials!" Nuptials. Sounds like something you get a case of. I felt a case of the nuptials coming on so I had a full-body fiancé. I lugged the basket to the shower, where it was my duty to create a hat out of discarded gift-wrapping ribbons and a paper plate.

"Take this." Francine tossed a circle of thin white cardboard into the basket lid. I put down my load, picked up the plate, and headed toward the buffet table.

"No"—she spun me around—"this is the basis for *le chapeau* you have to make me."

Please. *Le chapeau* you have to make me, *please*.

With no seats left, I plopped down on the floor and ripped a hole in the center of the plate with my teeth. I watched as thirty grown women feigned enthusiasm over a salad spinner. Sitting at Francine's feet as she opened her gifts, I felt like Santa's prized elf and began to take my hat construction very seriously. I crafted under-neck ties and strategically placed bows tied to the front of the plate so as to foster ideal plate-to-skull balance. I pretended to know things about physics. I pretended to know things about design. I pretended this was fun. So intent was I on creating the world's best bow bonnet, that the average partygoer would have mistaken me as an impeccable girlfriend. I even had the fleeting thought that this was a headpiece twelve-year-old Francine would have worn with pride.

When the hat was almost ready to wear, I spotted a long sturdy-looking ribbon that would have turned my crafts project from a hat to a work of art. It was dangling from Francine's chair and she was sitting on it. I considered my options and, having decided that the ribbon and I had a date with *le destiny*, yanked it as hard as I could out from under her. Apparently the ribbon had its own destiny to fulfill. The front of Francine's wrap dress fell gaping open, transforming it into a plunging neckline worthy of double-sided tape. She screamed in mock horror.

"Thank goodness it's just us girls!" exclaimed her mother.

I decided that the hat was good enough.

For the remainder of the shower, I took solace in a feast of mini bagels, mimosas, and cookies glazed to look like wedding bells and then covered in those gunmetal candy balls that give you rat cancer. Cast from unholy molds, there were also white chocolate brides-on-sticks. Bridal pops. As the chorus of women cooed at the unwrapping of a Crate & Barrel spice rack I caught a glimpse of Francine's great-aunt on the loveseat, gnawing at a bride's head with her gums. I lifted my plate of refined sugar and gave her a knowing wink but a cataract prevented any reciprocation. I became intensely jealous of her toothless grin and low-grade halitosis and the solitude it afforded her in a room full of vibrant women.

After the shiny exoskeleton was ripped from every box, I was summoned to take an aerial picture of all the women in the room with their engagement rings. Francine put her hand proudly on top. It was a cluster of skin and diamonds. Shrieks of "Take one with mine! Take one with mine! Did you take one with mine yet?" echoed across the living room. They bounced between the family portraits with the bichon in bows and ricocheted off the giant paisleys on the wallpaper. Women reached for their cameras with one arm, while holding their place in the hand pile with the other. If I had any remote inclination toward marriage—not an unhealthy Bridget Jones fascination, but the fundamental idea of someday finding my other duck-billed platypus and maybe buying a bridal magazine for duck-billed platypuses—this would have been cruel. They lucked out when they handed camera after camera to me.

I have never pictured my own wedding. I do want to get married. It's a nice idea. Though I think husbands are like tattoos—you should wait until you come across something you want on your body for the rest of your life instead of just wandering into a tattoo parlor on some idle Sunday and saying, "I feel like I should have one of these suckers by now. I'll take a thorny rose and a 'MOM' anchor, please. No, not that one—the big one."

This philosophy works but it also prevents me from getting a clear visual on me-as-bride. I have seen wedding dresses and thought they were beautiful but have never taken that crucial step further of envisioning my body in one. I have never scouted locales or eyed cakes through bakery windows. The one time I stood near the engagement rings at Tiffany, I got yelled at for leaning on the glass.

I guess my bridal party fantasy would have all my close guy and girlfriends sharply dressed and sitting in the front row with my family so I could look out and see them lined up like a collection of Pez dispensers. Maybe they could wear a lace ribbon of solidarity on their shirts, as if marriage were a cause and my wedding the cure. The only bit I have pictured in any detail is the music (maybe "The Book of Love" by the Magnetic Fields. Or Johnny Cash's "It Ain't Me, Babe"). It doesn't matter if the selection is slow or fast, but couples shouldn't scramble to select it. If you have ever gone dancing or on a road trip or had a romantic bout of serenaded sex on a winter night, you should have a few to pick from. If not, you probably shouldn't be getting married.

Out of a hat (literally—there were strips of paper involved), Francine had chosen "When Smoke Gets in Your Eyes."

When smoke blows up your ass.

Then, sometime between the shower and the wedding, the disaster happened. An e-mail arrived from Francine. It began, as all e-mails pertaining to this event did, with a "Ladies:". Ladies. Large masses of girls are often prone to this salutation. Once is fine, twice is acceptable, any more than that and I feel like I'm having high tea at Windsor. I hate being mollified with this unsolicited "ladies" business. I know we're all women. I am conscious of my breasts. Do I have to be conscious of yours as well?

Do men do this? Do they go "Men: Meet for ribs in the shed after the game. Keg beer, raw eggs, and death metal only." I would imagine not. I vowed the next person who addressed me as "ladies" in rapid succession was getting a Stuart Weitzman shoe shoved up her taffeta.

The e-mail suggested that we all get together for a last-minute bachelorette party the following night. Mixed drinks, penis quizzes, plastic tiaras, the works. But I had unbreakable plans. Plans I had made months before with a friend who was leaving the country for two years and with whom I had actually spoken in the past decade, on multiple occasions no less.

"I know this is a once-in-a-lifetime thing for you," I e-mailed my apologies. "But also once in a lifetime: one of my closest friends moving to Addis Ababa."

Francine called again, this time with the double agenda of logistical and emotional concern. She renegotiated. Since I was unable to attend the impromptu bachelorette party, perhaps I'd be interested in a long and pricey train ride to Boston to stay on her pullout couch and meet her fiancé? Say, this coming weekend? Or maybe I could get the whole week off work?

"I just want you to meet Boris and spend some quality time with him before the wedding," she pouted.

I felt guilty not giving her the bare minimum of what she needed. How inept at this bridesmaid stuff could one person be? But it seemed she "just" wanted a lot of things lately. Every request was minimized to the maximum (see: "I 'just' think it would be great if you wrote a poem in iambic pentameter for the candle-lighting ceremony"). Yet, even for her, she was disproportionately and irrationally upset. The kind of upset that incurs visions of Leslie Nielsen slapping a hysterical passenger à la *Airplane* while nuns with baseball bats wait in line to do the same.

"I'm so sorry. I know, maybe if I had more notice I could have—"

"I want you and Boris to be as good friends as we are!"

It was time to put my foot down. Or at least my toe. I've never been particularly fond of Boston as it is, having been dragged to Cheers as a child and nearly falling out of a swan boat. It's also too many white people in fleece, too many inconvenient modes of transport, too much Big Dig. It would take the love of my life being there for me to go. And Francine was not the love of my life. She was the love of this Boris person's. She didn't need me. Then, as I was at last ready to stand up and put an end to this just-add-saline bonding, she stopped me in my tracks with: "I only wish you could be there since you're the maid of honor."

"Horror" is a six-letter word. So is "fuck me." For all my female friendship foibles, I do posses an instinct or two about my own kind and I knew, as sure as you can know anything, that you *can* say no to being maid of honor. It's a job. People have turned down jobs before. I asked her, as gently as I could, when I had ascended to the throne. She said that I had inquired if there was a maid of honor months ago during one of our small talks about big things. She had said there wasn't one and I had replied quickly—like a nail being driven into a coffin with a single stroke—"Good to know." Three. Little. Words. How could I have allowed such massive fuckuppery to occur? I kept her on the phone as I looked on her wedding website and she was right—there I was, "Sloane Crosley, Maid of Honor, Francine's Best Friend." Apparently she had her own mental Rolodex and I had been misfiled in it from the beginning.

I suppose, considering the fact that it takes only three little words to express affection and two little words to legally consent to marriage, her reasoning was plausible. Still. I wondered if all her life's decisions since I had known her had been based on such subtleties of conversation, and it took everything I had to stop from asking, Are you *sure* you're engaged?

What an atrocious maid of honor she must have thought I was. I didn't fold so much as a single paper crane for her. I apologized repeatedly and profusely about not coming up to Boston. Eventually she forgave me and, unable to attend the four lunches in the week leading up to the wedding due to a violent case of fake mono the likes of which my person had not seen since the AP biology final of '95, I did force myself to heal for the rehearsal dinner. While it is important to develop something chronic at times like these, the rehearsal dinner had an air of nonnegotiability. I healed fast and even managed to regain the weight I had lost during my bout of faux glandular fever on the drive over.

Despite being five minutes early (thank you, Dad), I was the last of the bridesmaids to arrive. When I walked into the restaurant in downtown White Plains, Helen was there to greet me. She had sprained her ankle on a trampoline the day of the shower (an injury that struck me as so unusual I had the flickering hope that Helen was trying to get out of these wedding events as well).

But I knew this was Helen because she wore a shirt that read "Parallel Bars" and had a silk-screened picture of her and some drunk gymnast friends. And because she called me "Thloane."

ME (shaking her hand): Good to meet you, finally. I feel over-dressed.

HELEN (hugging me): You're not overdrehthed.

We entered a room set aside for private parties such as ours. Colorful obstructions called "flower arrangements" took over the tables. The walls were painted to look like the pre-9/11 Manhattan skyline. From the way the flat perspective-free buildings and their yellow squares of light were painted, one could argue that this was also a pre-Renaissance skyline. The ceiling was low, as was my tolerance from previously staying with my parents for a week. I spotted an open bar approximately 9.2 feet to my left. Francine galloped over to me and pulled me into a group of bridesmaids. I had met Stacy at the shower. I nodded and smiled at her. She blinked at me stoically, her eyelids caked in purple.

"Ladies," Francine said. "Ladies, I have an announcement to make."

Oh, my sweet Jesus, she's with child.

"Ladies, after much consideration, I have decided not to take my husband's last name."

On the one hand this news was bizarrely comforting to me and on the other it was fittingly disturbing. Not taking the husband's name is a traditionally untraditional move on the free-spirited bride's part. This was the old Francine talking. However, this has become a bit of a fad within an antifad and was commonplace enough that I didn't think it warranted three "Ladies." I guess if I had a third hand, on that one I wouldn't really care either way. But then intrigue began to percolate.

"The thing is"—she leaned in, conspiratorially—"I'm not keeping mine either."

I had a vision of Boris and Francine with no last names, falling off the grid somewhere in Idaho, living off the fat of the land, forgoing utensils and property tax and having a dog named Bark and a kid named Slipper Bubble. The most vividly imagined portion of this scenario came when I realized this meant they'd have no U.S. postal address and I wouldn't have to send a wedding gift. I smiled. Francine grabbed my hand and jerked it toward her.

"Isn't it great? We're going to be Mr. and Mrs. Universe."

"Like, hypothetically?" I said. "As in 'of or pertaining to the world'?"

"No." Her fingers were boa constrictors around mine. "As in 'of or pertaining to reality.' We're changing our last name to 'Universe.'"

"Francey, that's amazing!" Stacy squeaked like a dog toy.

I laughed very hard. Wine shot up into my nose, which I decided was God's way of telling me it was time to switch to hard alcohol. It quickly became apparent that I was alone in my amusement when all the women stopped chattering and looked at me like bunny rabbits.

"I mean . . ." I stammered and punched Francine on the arm with my free extremity, "ha! Good for you. Way to buck the system."

I got up to get a martini. I had questions. Unaskable questions. How was it that I actually knew someone, however tangentially, who blithely named herself after a trillion bodies of burning gas? What did her parents think? His? Is it even legal? Was "Universe" not a touch on the unabashedly self-righteous side? What, the "World" is not enough? Furthermore, if they had a baby and that baby was a girl, would she automatically win the pageant? Or maybe they'd give her the tiara but not the cash prize and list of duties?

But all those questions could wait, because I had the one thing that would carry me through the mundane small talk of the rest of the night. I had the one thing that would make my brain hurt less when I struggled to recall amusing anecdotes about Francine for her relatives from Missoula, the one thing that would allow me to tolerate Francine smacking my hand when I bit my nails, the one thing that would bring me comfort later that night when I was crouched over the toilet like an Olympic skier and violently ill from too many martinis mixed with shrimp gnocchi in vodka sauce.

I had her new initials. F. U.

Sleeping in my parents' the night before the wedding, I took stock of my childhood bedroom—a hermetically sealed vault with the exception of a defunct NordicTrack and a box of padded dry-cleaning hangers. I was bored. I was drunkish. I thought of a high school report I did on the Belgian artist René Magritte and a quote I once read from him, something about his favorite walk being the one he took around his own bedroom. He said that he never understood the need for people to travel because all the poetry and perspective you're ever going to get you already possess. Anaïs Nin had the same idea. We see the world as we are. So if it's the same brain we bring with us every time we open our eyes, what's the difference if we're looking at an island cove or a pocket watch? These people must have had bigger childhood bedrooms than mine.

Though I don't know the precise square footage, I do know that it wasn't meant to be a bedroom but a study of some sort. Or a kingdom for hamsters, which is how I used it. You can't lie down in my room and point your toes without touching furniture on both sides. And this has been true since I was twelve. I remember having a conversation with Kenny Stein, a short kid who moved into a house identical to ours but two streets over.

"So"—he came up to me on the playground with a kickball under his arm and a yarmulke on his head—"big or small?"

"Excuse me?" I was sitting with a group of girls I wanted to impress so it came out "Excuuuuuse *me*?"

"Big or small bedroom, yo. Which one you got?"

Kenny's family was from Missouri and he was eager to practice his regional diction.

"Oh." I looked away from his distractingly different-colored eyes, which because of his diminutive stature were on level with mine. My older sister had the real bedroom, the one with the little hallway, the walk-in closet, and the two full-sized windows. Kenny was an only child.

"Small." I shrugged as if my parents had offered me the big room but I had turned it down for Buddhist reasons.

"Ha!" he said. Then he spiked the kickball against the concrete touchdown-style and marched off to join his new friends, who would eventually turn on him and stuff him head first into a tire swing.

I turned the lights off and lay down on my old twin bed. I began counting glow-in-the-dark stars until my brain felt like the sand whirling in a hula hoop. When I was done, I turned the lights back on. I played with some tennis trophies, flipped through a plastic-covered dot-matrix report on the major exports of Bulgaria (textiles and cheese), and sniffed and threw out a dried corsage. I tried to do sit-ups with my calves on the bed. I reached up to a high shelf with a pile of more vellum-covered dot-matrix reports on subjects ranging from the life of the sea anemone to that of F. Scott Fitzgerald. They fell past my head and onto the floor with a surprising thud. I looked down to see my high school yearbook facedown and spread open on the pile. Huh, I thought, so there that thing is.

I picked up the postprom picture of a group of girls at the beach. It had slipped out of the inside cover. Standing there in the sand, with our arms around each other, we all looked so effortlessly unified and I became deeply envious of past me. It seemed that having girlfriends was a sign of innocence and a boundless capacity to care about other women. The hearts in that photograph had multiple strings attached to multiple other hearts. Everything was less about cliché and more about camaraderie. We weren't out for ourselves, we were out for each other. When had I forgotten that? When had I cut the pink wire?

When I woke up the next morning, my head radiating pressure, I swore I heard my alarm clock say, "You're not eighteen anymore, jackass." In the light of my bedroom, I took a second look at the photo and saw that we were all grimacing. I suddenly remembered the cattiness, that some of us were barely speaking to each other while others were speaking too much behind turned backs. Our faces were scrunched up against the glare of the sun, smiling because someone had no doubt told us to smile. I am holding car keys in my fist. We're just about ready to pack it up for the day, find our shoes in the sand, toss tepid bottles of water into the trash, and say good-bye for the next decade.

We see the world as we are.

In the movies, brides cry of joy on their wedding day, sashaying down petal-covered aisles in six-thousand-dollar dresses. In real life the crying comes way earlier, usually in the confines of a bridal suite bathroom, and results from the stress of a bouffant gone awry or a missing mother-in-law. The six-thousand-dollar dress, much to the dismay of child laborers everywhere, is real. Francine noticed that two pearls beneath her armpit had fallen off sometime during the course of the day. She started breathing heavily and had us scour the bridal suite and then the entire hotel for any sign of them. What, I thought, a six-thousand-dollar dress and no plastic pouch of spare thread and beads? I nearly went blind, getting rug burn on my knees from the heavily patterned hotel carpet. Like a starved man crawling through the desert, I'd think I see pearls everywhere when there were only balls of lint and, in one instance, a Tic Tac. Didn't they ever steam clean this place? Also, they weren't real pearls.

But no matter. The bride on her wedding day is like a giant eggshell of emotional turmoil ready to crack and turn this whole feast of love into a trauma scramble. And the unstable bride is that much closer to the frying pan. Modern cinema makes allowances for this kind of bride as well, largely in the romantic comedy format, where the portrait tends to be far too generous with her. In real life, the five-alarm freak-out comes not from cold feet or anything having to do with something silly like the actual prospect of sleeping with the same person for the rest of your life. It comes from not wanting to look puffy in posterity.

This is where the bridesmaids come in. We are to have an innate understanding of her fragility. We live under the constant fear of "ruining the wedding." Weddings don't get damaged, they don't get mediocre: they get ruined. One lost limo driver and the entire day goes from Zero to Destroyed faster than you can say Swarovski-encrusted Vera Wang. To have a traceable part of the destruction is a high crime against the highest order of femininity. One is not allowed to complain or object or give one's opinion ever, especially when directly asked for it. I, I was a poor candidate for this.

After getting our nails done at a place that criminally charged eighty dollars for manicures and pedicures (I inspected the finished result for flecks of gold leaf only to find nothing), we were off to the hair salon. I had forgotten what it was like to have my hair done in White Plains. My senior year of high school a mall called the Westchester opened with a Versace, a Burberry, and a Red Door Salon lined up on the first floor like kernels of corn on a Venetian marble cob. But we were on our way out, off to college or rehab or both, when these new avenues for shoplifting were putting down their roots. Many of us had jobs there, including myself, but there wasn't a whole lot of reflection done in between paychecks. We didn't think about what was to come. While we were away, the expansion continued—new stores opened in the mall and the Bloomingdale's down the street doubled in size. A Fortunoff's went up, followed by a Whole Foods, followed by, understandably, a Container Store.

But that is now and this was then: growing up, pre–Elizabeth Arden, my mother cut my hair over the kitchen sink rather than take me to the Galleria (where legend had it, some girl was raped in the food court) or the White Plains Pavilion (which held the DMV, a sushi restaurant called Panda Empire, and a Mexican restaurant called Salsa Town—in typical suburban fashion, the Japanese got an empire while the Mexicans got a town somewhere on its borders). I guess I should have known that Francine would have the same degree of awareness as I did. Surely perfectly reputable salons had opened across the street from places we used to go on avenues we used to turn down, but who knew anything about them?

With none of these new possibilities in mind and kitchen sinks not being five people wide, the mother of the bride booked the entire bridal party at the Garden of Desires salon, located on a low-grade highway of strip malls and car dealerships. A tiny place with floor-to-ceiling glam shots from the '70s visible through purple-tinted windows, it had the kind of surprising but mandatory valet parking you'd pay not to use. We checked in at the main desk beneath an airbrushed rendition of the Sistine Chapel. This is when Francine whirled around in anticipation of the gratitude she was about to receive as she announced that anyone who had come in from out of town for the wedding would be "taken care of." I wondered if the phrase had ever been used with anything but extreme malice within the walls of the Garden of Desires salon before this moment. I also wondered if coming in via commuter train qualified as "out of town." All of the women burst into spontaneous applause, including a cousin bridesmaid whom I happened to know still lived over her parents' garage in Scarsdale. I swiveled my head back like a bird of prey and furrowed my eyebrows at her.

"What are you doing?" I mouthed.

"Rolling with the punches," she said through clenched teeth, loud enough for only me to hear.

My stylist's name was Cindy. Cindy had the kind of hair that reminded me of a story I once heard about a Catholic girls high school in the Midwest. The entire senior class had to have their yearbook photos retaken because all the girls' bangs were so high, they got cut off in the pictures. The girl who told me this story was ten at the time and from rural Illinois. The story was told in defense of her own bangs, a tsunami wave of hair, frozen in midair never to crash, like a Japanese political cartoon. Cindy reminded me a little bit of her as well.

"So what we doin' today?" asked Cindy in a thick-as-cheesecake central Long Island accent. She spun me around in her chair and cut off the blood flow to my head with a giant bib. Then she spat gum into my hair.

"What the——?"

"It's fine, sweetheart," she said, holding up her hand to show me the gum in her palm. Then Cindy started attaching a claw-shaped item to a nuclear missile that plugged in and called itself a hairdryer.

I said: What are you doing?

She said: Drying your hair.

I reached up and felt the top of my head.

I said: But it is dry.

She said: I know that.

We were silent like an old Western film before the shootout. I thought I saw a tumbleweed blow past in the mirror. Then I realized it was some satisfied client's head. This was bad. Cindy and I were having communication issues at such an early stage in what was to be a meticulously scheduled three-hour rela-tionship. After a series of diplomatic questions in which I re-peatedly deferred to her infinite hairstyling wisdom and to which, Cindy being Cindy, she saw right through and became exasperated, I ascertained that she wanted to straighten my hair in order to put it up. Shampooing would apparently cause it to dry out.

"But if it's already dry——"

She cut me off, firing up the missile.

"Wait, wait. What if you don't shampoo it but just...use conditioner?" I suggested.

And that is how Cindy and I reached the compromise that was to make things much worse for me in the end. At the time I was quite proud of my hostage-negotiating skills. I felt like I had talked myself out of getting mugged by convincing my attacker to put down her gun and splash vinegar in my eyes instead.

Cindy hosed my head down and slathered me with stripper-scented oils. Then she put a megaphone attachment on the dryer and turned it on. In under an hour she burned the fleshy curl of both ears numb, a power I had previously thought was exclusive to ice cubes. In the end my hair hung so that the tips of my ears stuck out through it like a hobgoblin's. Cindy poked a new hole in the ozone layer spraying my follicles into place and stabbing me with forty-two bobby pins (I counted them after the wedding, when their journey away from my scalp was just as quick, violent, and painful as their journey toward it). She topped the whole thing off with a clippy-claw thing whose proper name and genus I do not know.

"Is it possible to use a bit less hair spray?" I coughed.

"Honey," she said as she leaned in, grabbing my shoulders from behind, "less hairspray? That's like asking a duck not to quack."

With that, the question-and-answer portion of the hair appointment was over. I glanced over my shoulder to see other members of the bridal party getting curled and colored, teased and smoothed, until they were each at least two inches taller. Francine was getting small silk roses and extensions wound around her head that made her look like a windblown Princess Leia. She chatted on her cell phone. "No, but I'm serious! Someone has to tell her to stop confusing food with love . . ."

Cindy put her nails on my cheeks and snapped my head to center. I thought about how if I saw a duck and it was really annoying, I think I just might very nicely ask it not to quack.

A can and a half of Aqua Net later (Me: "Didn't they discontinue that stuff?" Cindy: spraying sounds) when I looked adequately enough like a poodle-peacock crossbreed, Cindy undid my bib and released me.

"Turn around!" the other girls oohed and aahed in unison. You would have thought there was a salad spinner pinned to my head.

I knew what they were thinking, having thought it myself numerous times. I have seen something on another woman—a sweater or a hairdo or a new pair of glasses—and because it is so heinously ugly that I have been overtly staring at it, I have no choice but to compliment it instead.

That's when the music started. With Francine's hair finished, "Going to the Chapel" came on full blast through the speakers so used to channeling light rock. All the stylists dropped their curlers and straightening irons and came rushing over to sing and clap. The other girls started singing and clapping, too, like an off-Broadway musical. Way off. Francine smiled nervously; even Mrs. F. U. was embarrassed by this display. The three customers not tied to the wedding began clapping in their chairs and putting their hands to their hearts. Cindy got in on the action, dramatically waltzing with Francine. Others took turns. Who knew that "Going to the Chapel" is longer than "Stairway to Heaven"?

After the kooky older ladies had had their way with her, Francine was left standing and swaying and waiting for the song to be over. I watched her on the middle of this makeshift dance floor, upswept hair trimmings at her feet, and I stepped in to dance with her. Perhaps I had been imbued with an instinct for female herding over the past few months because suddenly the sight of a woman by herself seemed . . . unnatural. Either way we were both relieved. Her not to be swaying awkwardly to the City of Las Vegas theme song and me to understand for a split second what it was like to be in her pristine white shoes. I, too, was a single girl who spent her life standing and smiling and swaying and, sure, hoping someone I care about will dance with me, but more than anything? Hoping that this cheesy music will stop. As the song ended I dipped her for the benefit of everyone around us. The women cheered. Somewhere a flash went off. Francine looked up and mouthed, "Thank you."

"Any time," I lied.

The wedding was un-air-conditioned. The ceremony, though technically brief, felt like an eternity with hair spray—contaminated beads of sweat dripping into my eyes. I kept winking at the priest. I tried to turn away and found myself winking some more at the most innocuous wedding-goer I could find: Francine's great-aunt in the front row. A few rows behind her sat my parents, whose presence robbed me of my "least likely to be at this wedding" superlative. My mother, in a linen suit, spent the majority of the ceremony with her head down, rotating her rings and trying to smooth out the wrinkles left over from crossing her legs. My father, in an ill-advised wool suit, looked shiny and supportive. My feet hurt. I'd seen earlier a tray of mini quiche being carried into the reception hall. I have never longed so profoundly for mini quiche as I did that day. When the priest pronounced them Mr. and Mrs. Universe, I searched his face for signs of exasperation.

Besides my new bestest girlfriends and my parents, who were trapped talking to the parents of the groom, I knew no one at this affair. I took frequent trips to the bathroom during the reception for a little bit of solitude and lip-gloss reapplication. Almost every time I returned to the party, Francine could be found regaling guests with stories about the wedding planning. In each bit of distilled dialogue, a third party—a florist or a photographer or a matrimonial aura cleanser—would end up commenting on what a sane and happy bride she was. No bridezillas here!

She had asked us not to drink at the prewedding brunch, lest we bloat ourselves out of duty. As if we were astronauts, somehow owned by the government, which was somehow owned by her. The People's Republic of F. U. Needless to say, I felt that I had some catching up to do. I figured this was fine as, despite being crowned Queen of the Serfs, I had done some impressive foisting of the wedding toast onto Helen. In retrospect, it seems that there were better candidates for this, but it didn't occur to me at the time. When we discussed it earlier that morning—over a breakfast bonding session of mocha lattes in the new Starbucks—it was more of an electoral decision. Francine's constant assurances that this was not a bridetatorship had actually rubbed off and we didn't want to make the assumption that I would give the speech, did we? Just because my name was up in pixels on some dumb website? It was a girlishly democratic game of Red Rover and I made sure we sent Helen on over.

After all, who was I to talk the talk? What would I do—get up there and make a speech in which Francine's furniture fort–building skills as an eleven-year-old became a metaphor for life and marriage? Who amongst us has such talent to weave raw silk out of straw? But Helen, Helen approached Francine's marriage as it deserved to be approached: with the hovering enthusiasm of a hummingbird. The champagne glasses were clinked, the microphone was tapped. Helen looked radiant in her baby pink plaid. Almost as if Laura Ashley herself had thrown up directly on her. She tapped the microphone again and said, "Ith thith thing on?" And then she passed out.

No one knows why she went down like a sumo wrestler off a balance beam. The worst part of me thinks she faked it. The best part of me thinks she had planned on faking it from the beginning. Clever girl. Stacy and I helped her to a chair and got her water and bread rolls and maraschino cherries from the bar. I have never fainted before but it is my understanding that it almost always has something to do with blood sugar and it dropping. Francine shot up from the head table and covered her mouth but made no move to cross the dance floor. People held their champagne flutes frozen in midair. Helen staggered her way to vertical, holding her head with one hand and handing me the microphone. Stacy glared at me as if I had drugged Helen's white wine.

I held the mic and pulled a gold bamboo chair from a nearby table for Helen to sit on. When I went to give the mic back, she shook her head. Our little hummingbird looked like she had just smacked into a plate glass window.

"Take it," said Stacy with an unsubtle twinge of bitterness in her voice, "you're the maid of honor, aren't you?"

"That's my slave name," I snapped at her. I was intoxicated and ornery.

"You must be kidding me."

"Well, I'm not. But if you insist . . ."

"Go," said Helen, as if reaching out from a foxhole.

I assured the crowd that Helen was fine in a "these things happen all the time in the theater" kind of way. My position as maid of honor allowed me a certain level of authority, in this case medical.

"To Francine and Boris." Everyone raised their glasses even higher. "We just . . ."

I looked around the room at all the smiling and hopeful faces, most of which I didn't know and would probably never see again. My parents exchanged a look of grave concern. I sensed them plotting how to help me out of this. Maybe my father could fashion a large stage hook out of dessert forks and napkin rings. My mother stifled a giggle and mouthed, "Sorry, kiddo." My eyes fell back on Francine, who was preoccupied with a loose pearl on her left breast.

". . . it's hard to put into words . . ."

Weddings are friendship deal breakers if the friendship is weak. There are too many favors, too many tasks, too much required devotion and Aqua Net for imposters like me. I tried to make eye contact with Francine, to give her a knowing good-bye smile like the ghost of a loved one in a movie. It was no use. I decided to cut my final pink wire. There would be no more yearly "happy birthdays" and certainly no more bonding with the girl in the duct tape dress. That ship had sailed.

". . . we wish you guys a universe of happiness."

And everyone chuckled and drank and ate pink cake.

Recently I had lunch with another high school friend. One whom I see slightly more regularly than Francine because we live within a few miles of each other. Like my other female friends, she does not know my other female friends. But she did know Francine back when we were in our homegrown teenage cult, and I regaled her with the entire story.

"Remember Francine?" I began and I told her all of it. The call out of the blue that started it all, the ups, the downs, the Helens and the Cindys, the plaids and the stripes. Any compassion I felt for my middle school friend had evaporated, leaving little hard nuggets of infuriation. A symphony of insensitivity poured out of me, growing louder with every put-upon detail. As the priest said during the ceremony, "love is not boastful." But hate? Apparently hate has a big mouth.

Ironically, I was high on the key attraction of group female friendships that I have deprived myself of—collective memory. No back-story needed. When you have a steady and lifelong group of girlfriends, chances are the person you're telling the story to is actually part of the story. I never get to do this and, given the smallest taste, couldn't stop myself. When I stopped to breathe and take a bite of my food, my friend said: But don't you feel sorry for her? And I said: Sure, but my wallet doesn't.

We went back and forth like this for a while. Finally, feeling as if no matter how hard I tried, I wasn't aptly conveying the severity of my put-outness, I said, "I mean, it's as if you asked me to be in your wedding."

She smiled politely and dug into her salad, intentionally avoiding eye contact with me. We were both silent. I thought of the postprom beach photo tucked into my yearbook. She was there that day as well. In it, she's standing to my left and squinting like we all are but her smile is genuine as she grips the bare waists around her. I thought of the past and how one should have respect for it, like the elderly. I had known Francine for nearly twenty years. Had I no decency? I thought of britches bulging and bridges burning. My old friend continued smiling and glanced in the direction of the waiter. She had a piece of frisée lettuce stuck in her teeth. It felt cruel to tell her even this.

Then something familiar washed over me and I recognized it immediately as the same brand of girlish guilt that got me into this mess in the first place. You can't pick your girlfriend's teeth, but you sure as shit can pick your girlfriends. Oh, well, I thought, what's another burned footbridge between acquaintances? At least that's one less bridesmaid's dress I'll have to buy.

"Go like this." I motioned to my front teeth with my pointer finger. And then I paid for lunch.

THE HEIGHT OF LUXURY

The night before I turned sixteen, I was digging through my mother's jewelry box, pulling out old necklaces and the impossibly thick gold stickpins women used to wear on wool coats. This rummaging was a favorite hobby of mine, but on this particular evening I was digging with a purpose. I had caught wind of a surprise party to be thrown in honor of my burgeoning breasts. Teenagers are an unsubtle species, and the flood of seemingly random phone calls inquiring about my birthday plans led me to the only logical conclusion: surprise party. Plus, I had never been bat mitzvahed and I knew my parents felt I was owed a DJ and some Mylar balloons. I would need to accessorize.

I was not prepared to turn sixteen. My mother had taught me no female skills. I didn't know how to dress, how to use an eyelash curler, how to write in script (whereas they should create a font after my mother's handwriting). To this day I have no idea how to use eyeliner, but I am willing to forgo anything you have to sharpen before applying to your face. But I did know about jewelry. I knew what a cabochon amethyst was before I could tie my shoes. Like a featherless magpie, I was obsessed with all things sparkly. (My sister took the fixation one step further—she became one of the youngest patent holders in the United States when, at the age of fourteen, she invented magnetic jewelry clasps. She grew up to become a jewelry designer.) But my fascination with jewelry, specifically my mother's, was more sentimental than mechanical. I loved digging through her collection, asking, "Where's this from? And this one?" If I was lucky, she'd let me go down to the kitchen to retrieve the Bremner Wafers tin, which contained all her "special occasion" jewelry. Putting valuable things in the kitchen was a tip she'd read about in *Redbook* or an insurance pamphlet and it stuck. Should thieves have broken into our house and poured themselves bowls of cereal, they would have found all four of our passports.

My last evening as a fifteen-year-old, I had the Bremner Wafers tin between my legs on her bed. Suddenly I saw something roaming free and sparkly at the bottom of the tin. I pushed aside the rounded boxes and necklace sleeves to reveal a diamond ring I had never seen before. It was a princess-cut diamond, with two round stones on either side and a pink gold band that did not seem like something my mother would wear. I glanced across the room. She was at her desk with a bag of cotton balls, removing nail polish. I tried the ring on. I was unaware that people kept spare engagement rings. If they did, it seemed like something a sultan's wife would do, the height of luxury. We only lived in the height of suburbia.

"And this one?" I held up the ring.

"Oh"—she waved—"that's from Richard."

"Who the hell is Richard?"

"My first husband."

Now, it should be noted that my mother has a long history of being disturbingly unperturbed by what normal people deem perturbing. Certain things simply don't strike her as worthy of a sit-down. My first year of college, I went on a hypernostalgic rampage through the basement files, smiling at old photographs and science certificates from when it was still called just "science." (One day you turn around and "social studies" has become "Chilean fiefdoms of the fourteenth century" and that's how you know you're in college.) At the bottom of the drawer was a thin album of drawings I had done, including one (crayon on oak tag, age eight) of a teddy bear crying hysterically, wearing deely boppers and holding a windmill. In thick black crayon, I had scrawled the following across the bottom of the page: "Teddy bears are best because they understand it's nice to be alone." "Jesus," I said out loud, and brought the drawing to the kitchen table, where my parents were reading the paper.

"You didn't think this was cause for concern?"

My mother studied the drawing. "You were always kind of old for your age, if you know what I mean."

"Yes, I've heard that profound depression is a sign of maturity.

What if I had drawn four stick figures with no mouths and labeled it 'family'?"

"Oh, honey," she said, rubbing my back, "you were too talented for stick figures. You used to steal toothbrushes, though."

"That's right!" Now I was beaming, full of the kind of glee you experience when you remember last night's dream sometime past noon the following day.

My father looked up from the paper. "You used to steal our toothbrushes when you were angry with us."

It's true, I did. I bore the plight of the youngest like a pro. Not only was I the youngest of my immediate family, but of all the cousins in every direction. I often felt left out and if I was especially unhappy about it, I'd sneak upstairs during a holiday dinner, collect all the toothbrushes, and line them up at the bottom of my closet. Then I'd hang out with our cat, crack open the door, and watch the before-bed chaos ensue. So thrilled was I to have this memory back, at first it didn't occur to me that this, too, might have been cause for concern. My mother never thought to come up and look for me.

"I knew you'd come down in your own time."

"But I never did come down."

"For breakfast the next morning you did."

I could have been constructing toilet bombs up there. But this is her way. So the night before my sixteenth birthday she was only confirming what I already knew of her kookiness—it could strike at any time, most often in the form of nonchalance or forgetfulness. Still—never before had such pertinent information slipped through the parenting cracks.

"You never told me you were married before."

"I didn't? Huh. I thought I had."

"You didn't."

"I thought I had."

My mother's was an ironclad logic, impossible to penetrate. One would think a previous marriage would have come up over the course of sixteen years. One would be mistaken. It seemed strange to think of my mother's life before our little family. I was aware that she had one—a life—and a history as well, but never had it been brought into such sharp relief. I was aware of her past the way we are of the dinosaurs. Sure they existed, there's ample proof in the form of large, indisputable bones, but I have never imagined one alive—lightly snoring in the master bedroom down the hall.

They were divorced after fifty-one weeks of matrimony. Richard turned out to be a real prick. He was very into the barefoot-and-pregnant thing. Not that they ever had a kid together. That I know of. Maybe he just had a foot fetish, I don't know. They fought, he shoved her once, and he wasn't particularly fun at any time. He also tried to block the doorway when she left him. My mother ducked under his arm, ran to her car, and drove away. I remember thinking that this was somehow romantic, as it pinpointed the actual moment of my mother's departure, something you don't see a lot of outside television. Real people don't slam doors without opening them five minutes later because it's raining and they forgot their umbrella. They don't stop dead in their tracks because they realize they're in love with their best friend.

They don't say, "I'm leaving you, Jack," and fade to a paper towel commercial. She and Richard lived in Delaware and the law on the books in 1969 was one of those ancient east-coasty stipulations stating that if a woman left her husband, she was obligated to leave him with a bed, a chair, and a horse. My mother left him a futon, a giant beanbag, and the cat. They never spoke again.

I screamed for my sister.

"Dana, did you know that Mom was married before?"

"Sure," she said. She seemed annoyed to have been summoned from a conversation on her much-coveted private phone line. "To Richard."

"To Richard," I mimicked and tossed up my arms.

"Your father and I really did think you knew," my mother added, twisting the cap back onto the nail polish remover.

I wondered what else she might not be telling me. Was my mother a spy? A fly-by-night dominatrix? A Daughter of the American Revolution? Was there a dusty stack of wedding albums in the attic from all her previous marriages? Did Dad know? Suddenly it seemed that my mother's casual parenting was reserved for me. I had always chalked up my feelings of isolation as a child to being a child. What kid doesn't grow up feeling left out of the loop? Just being under four feet will do it. But here, under the same roof, was the perception of my mother as a responsible, basic-information-sharing human being and—albeit unintentionally—I was being left out of it. Again.

"Fine." I put the ring back in its mock-velvet box and shoved it in the can. "That's totally fine. You people call me when it's time to tell me I'm adopted."

With that, I marched down to the kitchen and heaved the family jewels back in the pantry. I got ready for bed, furiously scrubbing my eyeliner-free face and brushing my teeth like I was trying to erase them. I looked down at the three other candy-colored brushes, content to be in their holder. I spat into the sink. In less than twenty-four hours, it would be my big day. Hugs given, photos taken, secrets whispered. For one night only, it would be natural for people to tell me everything. I would have to pretend that I didn't see any of this coming, listening to competing tales from proud friends who fancied themselves spies in the making, thrilled by how slyly they threw me off the scent of celebration. I would be left out no longer. I practiced my "surprised" face in the mirror, a happier version of the "who the hell is Richard" face. I made a dramatic O with my mouth and put my hand on my heart. Then I put my toothbrush back in line with the others and went to bed.

SMELL THIS

"You can't really dust for vomit."
—This Is Spinal Tap

First, you must understand how to bake a successful dessert tart. Most baking, even complicated baking that results in caramelized pine nuts or perfect chocolate and vanilla swirls, consists of adding dry ingredients to wet. Any cookbook worth its weight in sugar will encourage you to experiment. Add craisins! Dally in dates! Go nuts! Perfection is to be found in the imperfect! Except with tarts. Unless you are a professional, you will find the tart to be a high-maintenance, unforgiving whistle-blower of a pastry. If they could sprout sexual organs and mate, they'd go extinct on the jungle floor. Chocolate chip cookies, impossible to fuck up, would breed like deer. Tarts are the red pandas of the baking Amazon. They are all about what you're not allowed to do. The crust alone: don't knead it too much too fast, don't sprinkle too much water, not *that* much butter, cool it first, don't cook it too long. This is a polite pastry. A civilized pastry.

Second, you have to imagine that your kitchen is a Manhattan-sized kitchen, itself a narrow island of a room. Let's say you have made a total of three tarts from scratch in the past. You have a supply of Crisco precisely for this purpose. You even invested in a twelve-dollar jar of pie weights, which was frustrating for you because "pie weights" are just rocks, but, this being New York City, you knew it was worth the splurge rather than going on a Clean Pebble Expedition in Tompkins Square Park. You think it's finally safe to feed your fourth tart to a few friends without poisoning them so you invite them over to your new studio apartment for dessert.

There are five of you in total. Two of your guests, a guy and a girl, you have witnessed having sex on several occasions, as they have been dating since freshman year of college and never saw a need to lock their respective doors. Because there are no more hippies, you don't call them hippies. (But if you ever saw two people on a beach, gorging themselves on whole-wheat burritos and pot, picking sand out of each other's toes, and diving into the water naked, that would be them.) Another girl, Justine, is a college friend as well. A Westport-bread WASP whose hobbies include water polo, impressionist art, cocaine, vintage clothing, and wandering through the history section of Barnes & Noble pointing out her great-great-grand relatives. Though you are probably closest to her, for months you've done little more than e-mail back and forth with jovial threats of getting together.

Justine brings along her new boyfriend, Trevor. Trevor the investment banker who is not an actual investment banker but works in finance. Since this is the only money-oriented job you come remotely close to grasping, you call everyone who works on Wall Street an "investment banker." You think he actually does something with hedge funds. Trims them, maybe. He has taken Justine golfing for the day and their faces and arms are burned Nantucket red.

You make a dark chocolate and pear tart with an apricot glaze. While poaching the pears, you press the dough evenly into the tart pan and let it chill for an hour while you tackle the chocolate. In a few years you will invest in a Cuisinart but for now you have unsweetened chocolate ground into your nail beds from breaking apart the stuff by hand.

As much as she'd like to, woman cannot live on dessert alone so you all go out to dinner first, to catch up. It's not that you have lost touch with these people. You haven't. It's just that they have kept in such close touch with each other. When scrolling through your cell phone, you generally let their numbers be highlighted for a second, hovering, and then move along to people you have spoken to within the month. It's not that you're a bad friend to these people. It's just that you're not a great one. They know the names of each other's coworkers and the blow-by-blow nature of each other's dramas; they go camping in the Berkshires together and have such sentences in their conversational arsenal as "You left your lip gloss in my bathroom." You have no such sentences. Your connection to your friends is half-baked and you are starting to forget their siblings' names, never mind their coworkers'.

But you're still in the play even if you're no longer a main character. Justine suggests a laid-back Italian restaurant down the street from your apartment, with designs on eating pasta and pale green salads with herb flecks in the dressing. Like the tart in the oven and your sparkling clean apartment, you think this is just perfect. The couple, Ryan and Mia, have come from a day in Brooklyn's Prospect Park, communing with pigeons and making origami for the homeless out of recycled coffee sleeves. Mia, wearing a Bennington T-shirt with the sleeves curled up, has not shaved her armpits since you've known her. She hugs you, asks after your parents, your job, your chi. Everything is punctuated with a question mark.

"We were making grass angels in the park? And there was this beautiful old oak tree? With lots of low branches? And Ryan thought he'd climb it?"

Justine, smoothing her hair back into a ponytail, keeps a rubber band in her teeth and waves with her elbow. Trevor is playing with some square of pocket-sized electronics that makes him laugh periodically. Otherwise he says nothing to you. Whereas at dinner, he talks nonstop.

"Lesbian sex is just hot." He chews with his mouth open. "No two ways about it—unless it's a three-way and then I'd be *all* about it."

You don't take much of a liking to Trevor. He winks at Justine, which is expected—half acknowledgment of bad behavior, half flirtation—who in turn apologizes to you for her boyfriend's behavior. You who did not deserve to get winked at over this. You are neither a practicing lesbian nor a close-minded prude nor have you ever had specific lesbian sex, namely with Justine. Thus leading you to deduce: Trevor wants to have a threesome with someone at the table and you are the only single girl there. You feel like telling him that you're not single in the way he thinks you're single. After all, you have yourself. You feel like telling him that if you were going to have a threesome with anyone, it'd be with earthy, fault-forgiving people like Mia and Ryan. You feel like telling him he has an oily blob of dressing on his chin that emphasizes the round wad of flesh at the root of his face. He shakes when he speaks, like a bowl full of Jell-O shots. You feel like telling him, "You know what, Trevor? No one here particularly likes you."

Out of nowhere, Trevor opens a tin canister of mustard with his thumb and shoves it in Justine's face.

"Smell this," he instructs, "it smells gross."

You have had enough.

"Have you ever seen lesbian sex, Trevor? Life-sized, unpixelated lesbian sex?"

"Why? Have you?"

"Because," you reason with him as he chews his cud, "I would imagine it's not all strippers with whorish tan lines in a pool somewhere."

"I get it." He sits back in his chair.

"What is it that you get?"

"You're Justine's 'arty' friend."

This actually isn't even true. Justine is Justine's arty friend. She knows more about art and art history than you do about pretty much anything. Even if she wasn't—what about Mia? The woman makes hand-painted lockets and three-dimensional paper dolls and sends them to tsunami victims. You couldn't even make a paper airplane to get them there.

"What's that supposed to mean?"

"That you're a feminist."

"Trevor," Justine pipes in, "a feminist is someone who believes in the equality of the sexes. Men are feminists."

"Whatever." He makes a face and digs into his linguini.

Perhaps it is the majority of your childhood spent at an all-girls sleep-away camp—bonding over campfires and head lice—that brings out your fierce loyalty to the lesbians. You spent your summers with more than one Mazzy Star–listening, celestial-ankle-tattoo-sporting, guitar-playing lady of sport. These were some of the deepest friendships you have ever known and, sure, some of that was before you grew up and learned about the oddly unique brand of friendship that occurs between gay women and straight women. But it doesn't detract from their value in your life. They say there is no such thing as gay or straight and that we all fall somewhere on the sexuality spectrum, as connected as kindergartners holding the same rope. You can get onboard with this. In fact, you are so onboard that you react with disproportionate malice to anyone who lets go of the rope—religious zealots, bigots, Red Sox fanatics, and small-dog owners. At that point, your personal beliefs are beside the point. Extremists and their supporters cause you to align yourself with something you're not in order to get as far away as possible from the something that you're *really* not. And right now you are Queen of the Lesbians.

"Why do you have to be such a fuckface, Trevor?"

You didn't debate the consequences of saying this beforehand but even if you had, you would have come to the sturdy conclusion that you will never see Trevor again. You see Justine twice a year as it is. Trevor stares at you. You think about excusing yourself to go to the restroom and instead sneaking out to buy a packaged Danish wheel from the Food Emporium. Trevor is officially no longer tart-worthy.

Someone at the table giggles the situation into tolerable. Trevor is the worst kind of asshole they make—the kind who is completely oblivious to how he sounds, the kind who is impossible to argue with because he doesn't allow for a worldview outside of his own. Normally, this wouldn't be a problem. Mean people happen. But with Ryan and Mia snuggling all hippie-like at the end of the table, you are left with Trevor *"The Da Vinci Code* RULES*!"* Shithead. After you get the check, Mia and Justine go to the ladies' room and you and Trevor walk out of the restaurant first. He walks ahead of you, tripping on some stairs and landing palms down on the pavement. He lurches to a standing position and wipes his hands on the back of his golf shorts. "Smooth move, Ex-Lax," he says to himself. You say nothing and walk past him. On the stroll back, Mia and Ryan link arms and laugh loudly. She makes monkey noises and he pretends to eat bugs out of her hair.

At home, as you pull out the dessert plates, you joke about college, telling stories about the catwalklike dining hall, stumbling drunk into the wrong room and innocently crawling into bed with people, European escapades involving cheap hostels and a stolen Peugeot. You are beginning to get the hang of these friendships again. They feel familiar, like riding a bike. This social ease could atrophy before the night is through. But for now, you're enjoying yourself. Justine watches over Trevor like he's her wolf cub.

The tart is too chocolatey. Not enough sugar. Flakes of crust huddle together where they were supposed to break apart. But it's edible. Justine takes a second slice.

During the course of the dessert each one of them gets up and goes to the bathroom. You do not recollect in what order, but none of them spends a memorable amount of time in there. It's getting late. You hug them all good-bye and walk them to the door, which was actually never out of sight in your apartment, but you walk them there anyway. After they leave you start scrubbing rings of chocolate and flour from the insides of bowls. You feel an abrupt pressure on your bladder and you head for the bathroom.

Now, living by oneself in a studio apartment, one becomes highly attuned to any minor changes. What would normally be pinned on a roommate becomes the work of the paranormal. You are the only culprit, the only one there to break things, leave underwear on the floor, forget to turn the lights out. The alternatives are unthinkable:

a. Burglar/rapists (an even worse prospect than model/actresses)

b. Still-in-the-closet heterosexual murderers

c. Vengeful spirits who hanged themselves from a light fixture in your apartment at the turn of the last century and who are back in the form of inconsiderate poltergeists that live in your IKEA couch cushions and finish off your cereal and then put the nearly empty box back without curling up the plastic inside.

For these reasons, your senses are heightened. You can immediately detect when something is out of whack. Nothing escapes the single-gal gaze. For instance: a perfect, cherry-sized turd on your bathroom carpet

Stage 1: Denial

Who shits on someone's carpet? Who does that? It's probably not even shit. Think of how immature you're being, assuming a chunk of unsweetened chocolate is shit. Think of how the other day you had a cab driver with the first name "Butt" and found it funny. Chastise your inner twelve-year-old, who is only supposed to rear her head in the face of kittens and swing sets. Be ashamed of yourself. It's chocolate or dirt, okay, but not feces. Apply this same kind of insta-denial a few months from now when you see a small roach scamper beneath your fridge. Think how you could just as easily have not seen the roach and gone on bragging about your hygiene, the way one does in New York. Who, me? I've never had a single bug, not one. The problem with the situation at foot is this turd ain't got no legs. It's just sitting there, staring at you, imprinting its image on your pupils. Or perhaps it's mooning you. Hard to say. But impossible to deny.

Stage 2: Scientific Identification

Because in this moment you still carry in your head the possibility of the turd being something less unholy—something you could point out to a toddler and say, "Look, a _____!"—because denial is dying but still has a pulse, you lean down to get a closer look. You must confirm that it is, in fact, chocolate. Or maybe raisins. The fact that the tart didn't include raisins is no concern of yours. In fact, there isn't a single raisin in the house but this does not deter you from getting on your hands and knees. You lean in closer to the carpet. (The carpet! Maybe if it was the tile, but the carpet!) Surely this is some type of cluster that fell out of a box or a canister, but not someone's digestive system. Despite your best efforts not to, you use your nose. It's not chocolate.

Stage 3: Suspicion of Origin

After rising at lightning speed to your feet so that you might have some personal space to shut your eyes and gag, you let your mind race through possible culprits. Your mind alights quickly on Trevor but keeps moving, deciding that this is the work of someone profoundly comfortable—perhaps too comfortable?—

in your home. Because you have a fundamental like for your other guests, because they are among your oldest friends, you entertain the possibility that a stray animal, such as a feral squirrel, has broken into your house, shat on your carpet, and left. In which case you have a bigger problem. Humans, you can simply not let in the front door again. A feral squirrel infestation is another matter. Then the idea of this being on purpose crosses your mind. How well do we ever really know our friends? And lately you've been a less than stellar one. You think back to July and Mia's birthday dinner you missed. You think of a long e-mail from Ryan so witty and detailed it deserved more than a two-line response. So you saved it for when your creativity was more flowy-like, but . . . did you ever actually reply? You don't think you did. Isn't this how domesticated animals act out when they're neglected? They piss on the carpet or gnaw at a favorite shoe? Perhaps these people have a point. Maybe that e-mail is still in your Drafts folder. Either way, you can't bake away the fact that you're a delinquent.

Stage 4: Honing of Suspicion

You remember that all four parties had spent the day outdoors, at parks and at golf courses. You are a shit detective. A regular Carmen Turdiego. You think of the nonhippie hippies, frolicking in the grass, rolling around like golden retrievers or burn victims, something getting stuck to the strap of a backpack or the bottom of a Reef flip-flop. You think of Justine and her boyfriend, their golf bags being dragged across what *looked* like mud.

You think perhaps you moved on too quickly from your first

instinct. Part of you would like to think it was Trevor. Let's face it, most of you would. The possibility of there being physical evidence of his awfulness beyond a few mildly irritating comments excites you. But would he really do this? You called him a name, yes, but wouldn't a little punitive tinkle on the toilet seat suffice? But if it was not Trevor, and not one of the other guests, than who? In a flash, you entertain the prospect that the shit doesn't fall far from the tree and, for dramatic effect, check your own shoes. Nothing, you're barefoot. Quick, go and put on some socks.

Sadly, none of it seems plausible. First of all, the turd is far too intact and shapely to have been crushed, taken out to dinner, walked home on pavement, and neatly deposited on your carpet. Second of all, you already established, back in Stage 2, that it would emit aroma if it were ground into a guest's clothes. Third of all, we are not wildebeests. The hairy mammoth is extinct. Fecal balls don't just "get stuck" to us and go unnoticed and unattended. You think of the word "dingle berry" and then again of the cab driver, Butt. You are riddled with shame and curious about whatever became of your swing set. Remember to call your mother when this thing blows over.

Stage 5: Revirginization
You wish the turd would vanish. You can already feel the association building between the turd and pear and chocolate tarts. Using no less than six sheets of paper towel folded on top of each other, you swiftly pick the shit up and flush it down the toilet. You throw the paper towel in the trash and get the trash bag out of the house. You then Lysol and vacuum up the memory of the

shit. You think, if you do this fast enough, it will be like it never happened. But all the spraying and all the vacuuming can't put everything right again. Days later, when you are still sidestepping the general region of the floor where the shit once was, you decide you can't live like this. It's time to launch Stage 6.

Stage 6: Investigation

There is no etiquette, no protocol for asking one's friends, "Did you by any chance take a dump on my floor after dinner the other night?" It's awkward. This seems obvious enough, but there are actually certain physical fallibilities for which polite society will allow. People sneeze in public, pee in the woods, burp into their fists, men adjust themselves, women get products that publicly compete to "stop leaks," they breastfeed, their children spit up on their blouses, and we shrug our shoulders. There's nothing to be done. This isn't Edith Wharton's New York. Nobody's perfect. We're only human after all. But shit on the carpet is so outlandish— so potentially hostile—suffice it to say, no one, but no one, is used to being questioned about it. It is utterly unbroachable. It's a far cry from "Did you just fart?" On the off chance you pass the first hurdle of putting such a question on the table, you then have the second hurdle of the answer. Who would confess to such a thing? (Professor Plum. With the turdzilla. In the bathroom.)

As you reach for the phone, trying to decide whom to call first, the worst part of the situation dawns on you. Statistically, what were the chances that no matter *how* the shit got there, the fourth person left it? What if the first person to use the bathroom left the poo ball and everyone who went in after has been thinking,

"Jesus, she's got shit on her floor." You comb your memory for the order, but find nothing. People tend to comment on how small your bathroom is. They usually say something like, "Your bathroom is really small." But even this throwaway remark cannot be fished out of the garbage disposal of your memory. Looks like you had too much wine at dinner. Apparently not enough to relieve yourself during dessert, but enough to lose sight of the bathroom processional.

You decide to call the least likely candidate to have left the turd but the most likely to have taken note of it. Your first tactic is to get comfortable by fishing for compliments.

JUSTINE: It was good, it was. You're too hard on yourself.

YOU: You don't think there was too much chocolate?

JUSTINE: Remember who you're talking to. There's no such thing as too much chocolate.

YOU: Oh, I think maybe there is.

JUSTINE: I ate two slices. Either way, it was good to see you.

YOU: Ditto. Did Trevor have fun? I'm sorry about the whole fuckface incident. I feel like this is the first time I've gotten to spend more than five seconds with him. Maybe I need to get to . . .

JUSTINE: Know him better?

YOU: Yes, that. Was he angry?

JUSTINE: Honestly, I wouldn't worry about it. I think he thought you were kidding.

YOU: Oh. I probably was. He's not lactose intolerant, is he?

JUSTINE: What a question. You know? I don't know. Why?

YOU: Some people are not tolerant of lactose. Good to know

if I do this again. Ixnay on the omemade ice creamay. What about sweets? Fiber? My cousin has a wheat allergy.

JUSTINE: I don't know what he's allergic to.

YOU: Sorry, just trying to think of others.

JUSTINE: Really? Are you feeling okay?

YOU: I'm good. You? Any gastrointestinal issues you'd like to share at this juncture?

This is not working out. You curse yourself for being so uninterested in the health of others on a normal basis that your present concern is highly conspicuous. You try Mia next. Something about her being another girl makes her seem like less of a candidate for baking up a nice shit cake and serving a slice of it on your bathroom carpet.

You call her on her cell phone, which she answers from the Fung Wah bus on the way to D.C. This girl opens her mouth and the words come out in the shape of grinning doll heads.

MIA: Hi, honey! Ryan and I had such a blast at your casa the other night? That tart?

YOU: So you digested the tart, then?

MIA: Huh?

YOU: You enjoyed it?

MIA: Yummyness.

YOU: Good, I'm glad.

MIA: We miss you! We have to tart it up more often!

YOU: That we do, that we do. Only thing is the cleanup. I must use every piece of kitchen equipment I have to make this tiny flat tart.

MIA: You could always make cakes.

YOU: Cakes?

MIA: You're a dessert snob. I love you, but you are! Ha!

YOU: I guess cakes would be easier to clean up. It's hard, in a small apartment, keeping everything clean . . . hygienic . . .

MIA (sounds of Chinese children in the seats behind her): Ryan has to bribe me with oral sex to get me to do the dishes.

YOU: There's a piece of information.

MIA: Hey, hold on a second. That's Justine on the other line.

YOU: Sure, go, go.

MIA: Can I call you right back? She sounds a little upset.

YOU: Oh?

MIA: Something about lactose and how she doesn't feel like she knows Trevor at all anymore.

Your fecal investigation is spiraling out of control and you need to rein it in. You decide not to call Ryan, the only other guest whose number you have. You're not sure why but you think it has something to do with the following: If it turns out he's at the center of Shittergate that will be awful and ruin what's left of your friendship. What will be infinitely worse, however, is if he's not the culprit and it remains a mystery.

In a few months, Justine will break up with Trevor. She will credit the night they came over to your place for dessert as the beginning of the end. You'll see each other on occasion. You'll have whole conversations on each other's voice mail until one day you won't. Eventually, you will run into Ryan in a park on the Lower East Side. He and Mia will be engaged and quitting their jobs to work on a Greenpeace boat. You'll say, "That's great," when the fact is you didn't know Greenpeace existed anymore. But this line of thinking will remind you that you need stamps. You will chat with Ryan for an appropriate amount of time and then an akwardness will descend.

During this lull in the conversation, you will plot a denouement in your head.

YOU: Ryan?

RYAN: Yeah?

YOU: About a year ago, did you happen to take a crap on my bathroom floor?

But before you open your mouth, you'll stop yourself. You will look hard at your old friend, your good friend, your friend who might be rescuing baby penguins or passing out bumper stickers this time next week. You'll wonder what you'd get out of knowing and at what price. You'll take a moment to think about the kind of person who is out to save the planet and hope that they couldn't do that if they were easily offended by the billions of people on it. You'll be grateful that a long time ago this kind of person chose to be your friend. But now you'll realize that even a person like this outgrows his friends. Even a person like this makes mistakes, can't always hold on to everything they'd like to, can't always force the world to spin in the direction of their choosing. You'll hug him longer than necessary and tell him to keep in touch. And you'll know, finally, that it had nothing to do with you.

LAY LIKE BROCCOLI

I am not a very good vegetarian anymore. There, I said it. Sure, I still like to veg out. Be still like vegetables. Lay like broccoli. But I used to be an exemplary vegetarian. A few years ago *The New Yorker* ran a cartoon of one woman explaining to another during a meal: "I started my vegetarianism for health reasons, then it became a moral choice, and now it's just to annoy people." Four people sent me that cartoon, including my mother. Who faxed it to me. At work. I grew to accept the fact that my refusal to eat anything that once had the will to crap was a source of amusement for others. And I learned to keep a set of (vegetable) stock answers at my disposal for all queries about my diet.

Most of your shoes are made of leather or suede. Why is that?
"Because I'm not going to eat my boots, that's why. There's a

big difference between stepping on something and making it a part of you. I'm not going to eat sidewalk either."

What do you mean "no meat"? No chicken? No lobster?
"Just venison."

Potatoes have eyes and you eat those.
No response.

The problem now is I'm not sure I have the right to champion the vegetarian cause. Not anymore. What follows is my journey into and back out of the temple of the seitanic. A roughage exposé, if you will. And I did.

The first thing to understand is that being a vegetarian is actually a pretty private matter. I am still taken aback by the question "Then what do you eat?" and am embarrassed as I struggle to produce the week's food diary. It's not that I'm ashamed of what I eat, but it's none of anyone's business. I imagine I would have a similar feeling counting up how many pairs of underwear I went through in a week. The only reason opening someone's refrigerator is more socially acceptable than opening someone's medicine cabinet is that people keep beer in their refrigerator.

As a lifestyle once kept between a select few and that now has many coming out of the freezer, being a vegetarian in New York is not unlike being gay. Vegetarian restaurants and options abound. I have the same number of veggie friends as I do gay friends. Because it's so common and often even hip to be a vegetarian, it's become socially acceptable to poke fun at us.

Being a vegan, of course, is more like the dietary equivalent of being a transsexual. Acceptance isn't quite as contagious as it should be.

I tried being a vegan once. Six months of tempeh and kale and I cracked like a rice cake and inhaled an entire box of fluorescent mac and cheese. It was just too hard for me to keep up the charade of a dairy-free existence. The surprising part was how easy veganism was to enter into. You read enough books that make *The Jungle* look like *Goodnight Moon* and you wake up one day to find yourself a recycled-paper-card-carrying member of the tofu mafia. And I knew which books to read, all right.

My own private Idaho potato went like this: When I was a teenager a renowned South African acupuncturist moved in next door to my parents. He and his wife (who pronounces "lime" like "lamb," thus leading to an infamous pie recipe debacle) are still the hippest couple my parents know and single-handedly responsible for introducing them to Trader Joe's and the Fugees. One day I told the acupuncturist I wanted to be a vegetarian. I wish I could remember why I wanted to stop eating meat, but this was high school and I also wish I could remember my motivation for drinking Zima and wearing flannel in public. I took the train into the city to meet with a nutritionist in the acupuncturist's office. She took my whim far more seriously than I did. She talked about tahini, how to cook vegetables properly, and the semiapocalyptic idea that you could soak almonds for days to make "milk." That I never tried. But I did buy a cookbook called *The Single Vegan*. A lifetime later, when I moved into my first apartment in Manhattan, I tried to buy another vegan cookbook—though I was eating cake and cheddar by then—and so I went to a used bookstore in my neighborhood where, oddly, they had only one title in stock: *The Single Vegan*. It made sense that the only guide to a vegan diet available in an area otherwise known for egg salad and whitefish would focus on the solo eater. The book was filled with lots of tips on eating for one, making barley and carrot pudding last a week. Who would subject their whole family to *that*?

Looking back, I should have taken my first encounter with *The Single Vegan* as a cosmic hint to be less of a high-maintenance eater—the soy cheese always stands alone. Instead I saw myself as this nutritionist woman saw me: a power vegan in the making. I juiced things. Lots of things.

For a while anyway. Damn you, delicious powdered cheese.

So that's my story of how I became a veggie—because I couldn't hack it as a vegan. Except now I can't hack it as a vegetarian anymore, either. What can I say? New York is sushi city, and sushi is the one thing I've consistently craved over the past decade (besides the secret craving of every vegetarian: bacon). My education about the moral and environmental impact of eating animals is thorough, but my response to all the statistics has developed a major fissure called "sashimi." At first I started with gateway fish: salmon and tuna. I think it's because when I pictured them, they were in massive schools where, going against the current of every crunchy article I had ever believed in, I reasoned: Would they really miss just one? Probably more convenient with one less car on the road. And wham: Now I'll eat eel.

In my lame pescetarian defense, it's very hard to be a girl and say you won't eat something. Refuse one plate of bacon-wrapped pork rinds and you're an anorexic. Accept them and you're on Atkins. Excuse yourself to go to the bathroom and you're bulimic. Best to keep perfectly still and bring an IV of fluids with you to dinner.

In fact, one of the more interesting results of telling carnivores you used to be a vegan but have switched back to vegetarianism is how much their reaction mirrors that of hard-core vegans. Suddenly you're caught in between the extremes and not satisfactorily passionate about your diet for either group. Carnivores, like vegans, can become incredulous, trying to find faults in your logic. If I'm going to start eating cheese again, why not eat the cow? How can I eat eggs if I'm not willing to eat the chicken? But instead of being convinced that I should eat the cow, I am once again convinced that I shouldn't eat the cheese. And all I can think is: You brought out every roadblock you could to keep me from going down this road. You judged, you mocked, you faxed me cartoons. Are you sure you want to encourage me to try again?

As for other vegetarians, I tell them I started eating sushi because I developed a mercury deficiency. I had to become a pescetarian to save my life. This is a total lie. But it's a lie that works. Contrary to popular belief, vegetarians aren't holistic Nazis. They will accept medical betrayal. What they won't accept is that I got lazy and decided fish were yummy and didn't have nervous systems complex enough to register pain, and that celebrities like Edward Furlong are freaks for trying to free the lobsters.

So what's to become of me now? Like anything that begins on the fringe, vegetarianism is dominated by older adherents who will kick you out of the veggie club faster than you can say "grilled vegetable terrine." With raw and organic food available in every zip code, we have it easy compared to them. Back in their day they had to walk five miles, uphill both ways, until their Birkenstocks were bloody, just to get a slice of polenta. They are quick to judge and would rather break bread with a veal eater than a nouveau fad vegetarian. I eat with the fishes so life is easy for me all of a sudden. Thus I have opted to keep my mouth shut about my dirty sushi secret.

The truth is I'm not particularly sure why I don't eat meat anymore. Any well-educated carnivore could easily thrash me in a debate on the subject—but not dissuade me. Meat (cows, pigs, Bambi) is the final frontier and I can't bring myself to cross it. Alas, I will continue to attend weddings where I have to politely pull the waiter aside and explain my situation. Without fail the exact same plate returns ten minutes later—a couple of string beans rolling in the juicy outline of a steak. Yes, my proclivity for the chickpea has staying power. And why? Habit. Habit and a stockpile of snarky anticarnivore comebacks.

Except now I have to be careful not to make them in the company of hard-core vegetarians. It's more acceptable to tailor your own religion (see this first-date classic: "I don't believe in God, but I do believe in something bigger than 'us' ") than it is to tailor your own vegetarianism. But if vegetarianism really is some kind of urban faith, this is me throwing my hands together and renewing my vows to vegetables. The words are secondary to the sentiment. Praise be to wheatgrass. Artichoke me with okra and baptize me in beet juice. Juices saves.

FEVER FAKER

There are few diseases for which the cure is objectively as bad as the affliction. Cancer is one of them. Crack addiction is another. Lucky for me, I didn't have either in the summer of 2005. There was no hospital wing or teen docudrama dedicated to my disease. There was no lapel ribbon for what I had. It was something you had to look up and shout twice in a crowded room before you were understood.

I was sitting at my desk at work, trying to click my in-box down to a point where I could at least see all my unread e-mails on one screen, when my doctor called. I had gone for my yearly physical the week before. I went to a very good Upper East Side doctor—the kind that gets mentioned in *New York* magazine more often than not and the kind that has an office with black-and-white pictures on the desk and signed prints on the wall. I remember thinking that it was unnecessarily kind of him to call and let me know that everything was fine with my blood test. What service! God bless him and the HMO that allowed me luxury box seats to my health for the bargain price of twenty dollars.

"Your iron levels are very high," he said flatly. "This thing reads like you've been chewing spinach in your sleep."

It's hard not to take it literally when medical professionals make analogies. I thought, well, had I? I don't remember chewing spinach in my sleep. Sounds bad for the jaw. At the very least, I would think it was a choking hazard.

"But that's good, no? People take iron supplements."

I pictured an army of anemic zombie girls storming my house in the night to steal my iron-rich blood.

"Well, no, not exactly. Too much iron usually points to a condition called hemochromatosis." He spelled it out as I scribbled on the back of a business card. "If left untreated it can ruin major organs, lead to heart problems, diabetes, death, etc."

What could be less et cetera than death?

"It often gets caught later in life once heart disease occurs and there's an abnormally rapid deterioration and no one can figure out why. Usually we say, 'Aha, she had hemochromatosis.'"

"If you had a dime . . ."

"Exactly. I'm going to send you to a hematologist to be sure."

I could feel my heart beating in my teeth. But he was breathtakingly calm. He had gotten good at this over the years. I was like some fuzzy animal and his voice was the pad of a human finger being rubbed over the bridge of my nose.

"Okay," I said, and got out a pad of paper, anxious to be part of the solution, "so how do we fix this? Pills, surgery?"

"You need a phlebotomy."

"*You* have a lobotomy."

"A phlebotomy," he said. "You get a quart of blood taken out periodically and it helps lower the iron levels."

As it turns out, "phlebotomy" is a fancy term for having blood taken. Though when it's done at a heavy rate to cure something, it's a fancy word for leeching. Where was my pill? What century was it again? I was prepared to have a mysterious and glamorous amount of prescription bottles in my medicine cabinet, but this was flat-out inconvenient.

"How often?"

"Usually twice a week."

"That's not so bad."

"For a year. If you were a man," he added, "I'd tell you to cut yourself shaving."

"And you think I have this thing?"

"I do. But I can't be sure. We need to retest you. You'll go see Dr. Spellman."

I hung up the phone and found myself lifting my hand to my face. I imagined it fading away like Michael J. Fox's in *Back to the Future*. I wiggled my fingers as bumper sticker–worthy slogans adhered themselves to my thoughts: "Blood. It's just *everywhere*." If I had broken my leg, that would be one thing. Isolated pain below my waist. But there was no escaping the mobility of liquid. I googled my new disease. There are lots of support sites, including one that sounded like a death metal band (Ironoverload.org), but the distinctly unsupportive CDC was my favorite. The ".gov" sucked me in from the beginning with the promise of seriousness and the possibility of espionage somewhere down the line. The CDC leveled with me. That last *C* stands for Control, not Cure, and certainly never Cuddle. I learned this the hard way.

Q: What can happen as a result of hemochromatosis?

A: Liver cancer, heart disease, infertility, diabetes, and impotence.

Q: Is hemochromatosis fatal if left untreated?

A: Yes. Yes, it is. You will be quite dead.

Q: Is it a rare and royal pain in the veins in the meantime?

A: Yes. You're in for it. This would all go much smoother if you were a cutter or a member of the hemophilia-prone bourgeoisie.

I closed out of the Web and rolled back in my chair. I breathed a giant sigh of relief. In a way, I had been waiting for this since birth.

I come from a broken home. My sister has Crohn's disease, for which she has been hospitalized. She also has heart problems, stomach problems, inner ear problems, a bad jaw, and a worse ankle. She went to many doctors in her teenage years, more than one of whom suspected hypochondria and suggested she see a psychiatrist, which she eventually did. Aside from the basic neurosis that comes with being a type-A personality in a grade-D-functioning body, there's nothing wrong with her. There's nothing that connects her dots—she's just broken. Once she fell and twisted her foot so hard, her Achilles tendon came loose and shot up into her leg like a rubber band. They had to cut open her calf to loop it back down. She got the ankle problems from my mother, who has scoliosis so severe it's resulted in pinched nerves, bone grafts, and migraines. During one of her more major surgeries she had two-foot-long metal rods inserted into her back.

The practical effect of all this on me has been that I am very comfortable with hospitals. I don't mind their veterinary smell or their big metal elevators or the scent of latex dust or atriums of any kind. The one thing I do mind is how glaringly healthy it all makes you feel.

One of the symptoms of having loved ones with multiple illnesses is guilt. There had never really been a whole lot wrong with me that was worth writing home—especially my home—about. My father and I tended to fly more or less under the disease radar. A flu there, a root canal here, but basically we kept our chins up, our mouths shut, and our urine clean. I perceived my secret desire to take one of my sister's ailments on for myself as normal. As an adult, I wanted one of my sister's sicknesses to unburden her. As a kid, my motivations were significantly less complex. Though my parents were almost freakishly even-handed with us, I wanted a bit of that get-out-of-jail-free sympathy thrown my way. For me it was always, "I'm sorry, I know you have the sniffles, but you have to go to school today." For my sister it was, "Brains leaking out of your ears again, darling? Let's get you some tea and see if there's anything good on TV."

It's strange, therefore, that I wasn't particularly into playing sick as a child. Perhaps I knew I couldn't compete. Just once I held an electronic thermometer in close orbit to a lightbulb and when I found that to be ineffective, I put the thermometer in the microwave for a reasonable number of seconds. I brought it to my mother lamely and dropped it in her hand, like a cat releasing a dead mouse. The metal end of it burned her palm.

"What happened to this thing?" she asked, poking at the 2,057-degree screen.

"I think it broke."

"Did you try to use it?"

Yes, I thought. Not only did I try to use it but it seemed grossly obvious to me that I had stuck it in the microwave.

"Nope. I pressed the little button and that's what it said. See?" I held the little stick with her. "It won't go back to zero."

I coughed, a neat cough like a chipmunk with clear little lungs. "I don't feel good."

"It won't even turn off," she said, holding down the Reset button with her nail.

"I think we should return it." I coughed again.

That was my first and last significant attempt at crying wolf. Though I have never been very interested in pity as a form of affection, seeing my sister brave her way through illness after illness, I have been tempted by the idea of a brave face. The kind of admiration my sister gets is a form of pity as well. It's like good cholesterol vs. bad cholesterol. She gets the good kind. It's a special brand of reverent compliment that is whispered behind the back, as in "She's just *such* a trouper," and followed close behind by its sister sympathy, "Poor thing." Though whispering around her is pretty pointless. If anyone knows about the echo quality of atriums, it's my sister. Not much gets past her when it comes to the complex terrain of pity. She would never admit to enjoying the "reverent compliment," but I have seen and been frightened by the venom she's prepared to release into the necks of those who have wronged her while she was ill. After the doctor's phone call, I have to say I looked forward to releasing some venom of my own.

I gave up on my morning of managing e-mail. I sat at my desk, ready to pick up the phone again. I wasn't officially diagnosed yet, but I knew this was the kind of thing that would interest my family immensely, being the diseased clan they are. Unfortunately, after a certain age, it becomes difficult to share any news with your parents that begins with "I have something to tell you" without sensing the hopeful expectation behind their voices: they want me to be a lesbian. That would explain so much for them—if I'm single, why I'm single; if I'm not wearing makeup, why I'm not wearing makeup; if I don't want to be set up with their friends' children, why I don't want to be set up with their friends' children.

My mother screamed for my father.

"Denis, pick up the phone! Your daughter has news!"

"Which one?" He clicked in.

"It's me, Dad."

"Hi, me. How can we be of service?"

I adopted my doctor's flat, professional, but easy tone and explained my situation as it had been explained to me: shock 'em with the diagnosis, comfort 'em with the cure. They were silent.

"Pretend I'm a superhero," I added. "Iron Woman."

"Well, hey," my father piped in, "maybe now you'll be able to set off metal detectors like your mother."

Now that I had told my parents, my disease seemed more real but less dramatic. These are people who come from the "call me when you're bleeding" school of sick days. Once my father sliced off part of a finger with a razor blade while redoing the wallpaper in our den. He sat on the sofa with this towel-wrapped hand in the air like a bloody Statue of Liberty while my mother set about expunging bloody splatters from her freshly purchased wallpaper. About two hours and four red-soaked hand towels later, it was suggested that perhaps a trip to the emergency room was in order.

I don't know why I expected them to waver from their "no intensive care, no problem" policy but I felt a twinge of disappointment at their lack of concern. Perhaps they had been worn down by all the very real drama of my sister's health. Perhaps they were merely trying to remain calm, sounding inner parental alarms so high-pitched only the dog could hear them.

I had given blood before, but never to a nurse at a blood doctor's office. It was like having that first sip of good vodka and tasting hints of what it is all the crappy vodkas are trying for. They painlessly filled up four different vials and sent me back to the waiting room where I did some filling of my own: at least ten double-sided forms. Long gone was the realm of primary care. Specialists were a different league of form. They asked me about every procedure I'd ever had. Piercings? Yes. Broken bones? Yes. Spinal taps? Actually, yes.

The week before I left for college, my mother took me to every doctor she could think of. Her empty-nest insanity had gotten the best of her and she temporarily forgot that Connecticut wasn't

Calcutta. We went to the dentist, the gynecologist, the ear, nose, and throat doctor, and the optometrist where she hovered as I rested my chin on a metal slate and flinched into what appeared to be an elaborate espresso machine. Through the hole in the center of the contraption, the doctor's eyeball was magnified. I focused on it and he flinched backwards. Then he shone a pen-sized flashlight in my eyes, said "huh," and left the room. He shut the door behind him and the room turned dark.

You never, or almost never, want to hear a medical professional say "huh" followed by a door slam. I picked at my nails.

"Don't pick at your nails," my mother scolded me in the dark.

"How can you even tell?"

"See! I knew it. I knew you were picking!"

The door frame lit up again. My doctor returned with another physician, who did the same thing with the flashlight and once again consulted the espresso machine. The first doctor explained to me that I had swollen optic nerves.

"They don't feel swollen."

"They are." He looked at my mother.

"Probably because of all that child abuse," she laughed.

My whole family likes to joke with doctors as if to say: I know we're your patients but we're one of you. You don't need to coddle us. We will not be big babies about our diagnosis. They have been known to stop seeing physicians who don't laugh at their jokes. I wholeheartedly disagree with this way of being. I am a big fat baby and I'm fine with that.

"What does that mean?" It was time to get serious. The doctor directed his answer at my mother as if I had thrown my voice.

"It means one of three things . . ."

I imagined three game show set frames with sparkling red curtains and my mother in a majorette's outfit drawing them back one at a time.

"She either has an excess of calcium deposits on the eyes, an excess of spinal fluid, or a brain tumor."

Ta-dah!

My mother had no jokes for this one. She held on to her purse like the doctor might steal it. Then he made eye contact with me for the first time.

"I don't have a brain tumor," I explained, almost inaudible. "I have freshman orientation."

And so I left for it. I grabbed a plastic cup, waited in line for keg beer, played mnemonic name games, and even kicked my legs up for "Crab soccer on the Green! One o'clock! Across from the chapel!" The sun was shining down on the grass, the mica-flecked stones of academia glistened in the distance. I walked on my palms, imagining the giant rubber ball as my brain tumor. I made such a herculean effort to keep it in the air, I could have been mistaken for a joiner. I went around the campus meeting people, shaking their hands limply, as chances were I had a malignant tumor the size of a grapefruit.

A few weeks later I returned to New York to begin ruling out possible causes for my fat-ass nerves. That's when I had the spinal tap. While not something I'd recommend for recreational purposes, it isn't horrendously bad. Mostly it's the lying naked in fetal position for two hours with a needle between your vertebrae and everyone reiterating that you are not to move under any circumstance. At no point does anyone come out and say it, but each warning is another nail in the coffin labeled "potential paralysis."

When the test results came back it turned out I had tiny calcium deposits on my eyes. Too much milk as a child or something. The calcium deposits caused my optic nerves to appear swollen. It was nothing to worry about. Just something to warn eye doctors of in the future so they didn't get CAT scan–happy on me.

I couldn't remember the last time I thought of my week of menacing death. I hadn't even considered it in the face of this new odd blood ailment. Medically, my new problem and my old were completely unrelated. But now, sitting in these waiting room bucket seats surrounded by old copies of *AARP*, *New York*, and *Hematology Today* ("Wonder what their circulation is like," my father might say for the benefit of the nurses), I could hear the voice-over: "Imagine you had one week to live. What would *you* do?" I could feel a familiar paralysis set in. Apparently, I would do nothing.

Anyone who was with me during that first week of college will attest to the fact that I didn't do a single upperclassman or one-handed keg stand or anything beyond the basic social requirements of freshman orientation. There are no voice-overs (if there are, that's a whole other problem) and news of one's imminent death tends to inspire profound upset, not reckless mania. It was comforting to know that in my highly abnormal state I was at least reacting normally to something. Still, I wondered if my new disease would inspire the same status quo attitude I had experienced years earlier.

"So, Sloane," the hematologist said as he peered at my chart. "Like the cancer hospital?"

I nodded.

"Don't tell me—Dr. Getty thinks you have hemochromatosis."

I nodded again.

"Yes!" he said. "I knew it!"

I remained stone-faced. If anyone should know how to read a blood chart, I thought it should be this guy. I wasn't prepared to congratulate him for this.

"And you're of Eastern European descent."

I felt like I was watching Dionne Warwick and her psychic friends sucker me into a hundred-dollar phone bill by telling me what I already knew. He went on to explain how the disease works, which nationalities are prone to it, and why iron buildup is a bad thing. While I am always appreciative of doctors who don't speak to you like you're an idiot, when he got to the advanced biochemistry of my blood cells it was time to say "uncle."

"You lost me at hemoglobin."

"We have to administer a more specific test. If your iron levels remain as high as they appear now, you'll have to be phlebotomized frequently."

"Is that legal?" I tightened my paper robe.

"Quite. And if this is the case, we should start soon. Best means of prevention. You can get dressed now."

Turns out I was wrong about the lapel ribbons. The green ribbon, though more commonly associated with organ donation and missing children, is also the choice of hemochromatosis-conscious lapels worldwide. Green was a reliably good color on me. Green I could do without drawing too much of the bad kind of pity while retaining the good kind of dignity. It was certainly better than brown (antitobacco, presumably cream-toned before all that Skoal), periwinkle (eating disorders, also the color of a Big Gulp in reverse), or my personal favorite—gray with black speckling (toxic molds, self-explanatory). It also turns out that my blood is type O negative, the universal donor. And because there was apparently nothing wrong with my actual blood, only the way in which my organs were processing it, that would mean I was giving about a pint of blood to the Red Cross every week. I figured at twice a week, this added up to enough good deeds to earn me a year of get-out-of-jail-free bitchdom.

Some people have water weight, I had blood weight. I was looking forward to losing it. I knew I was moving fast—I wasn't officially diagnosed but I found myself clicking back into the CDC website and further into the labyrinth of "symptoms" links. I felt my heart pounding, pushing out my metallic blood. I envisioned my red blood cells magnified and shaped like hemorrhoid cushions. I pictured them being doused in liquid mica on their way out of my arteries so that my blood actually sparkled.

The symptoms of hemochromatosis could include fatigue, nonspecific stomach pain, weight fluctuation, loss of sex drive, depression, and excessive urination. I had myself an explanation for everything that had ever been wrong with me. All I had to do was get used to needles and lay off the iron-stuffed sushi. The absence of eel and tuna rolls would have to be appropriately mourned but it was a fair trade.

My mind was a slide show, a trip down Ailment Lane: Me, pensive on a Fort Lauderdale beach during Spring Break. No Jet Skis for me, thank you; I've got my journal to keep me company. Me, missing the second half of *Chicago* on Broadway because I was trapped in the bathroom. You can see how I didn't even have time to cover the seat with toilet paper. Me at two A.M. after a night of drinking, scheming how to politely make an entire box of pancake mix and go to sleep rather than have intercourse with my boyfriend. Why, I had even been tired as recently as the night before! Just thinking about it made me yawn! I had a destiny and that destiny had a name and that name was hemochromatosis. I felt better already.

My sister wanted to come with me to the hematologist's office to get the results, but I wouldn't let her. Like a broken compass, here was a woman for whom all doctors pointed to something bad. She never left a medical office without a diagnosis for something fairly awful scribbled down and folded up in her wallet. Just being in the vicinity of a prescription pad was pressing her already bad luck. Not to mention that if I did have hemochromatosis, I didn't want her there. The one tiny detail I had not yet shared was that this thing was hereditary. While my parents were probably fine, chances were that she had it, too. All those years wishing I could take something on for her, and here I was about to give her one more thing to worry about.

Also: I knew I didn't have it. What I learned from my eye tumor fake-out was not so much "live life to the fullest" as "don't get your hopes up." It was perversely ideal: A disease that would enable me to leave work early twice a week? A disease that would get me out of any social situation of my choosing? A disease that would keep me in sugar cookies from the doctor's office for a year? A disease that I would never actually *get* as long as I kept up the cure? Another bumper sticker: "Too globin to be true."

I went to get the results by myself but I knew them before I walked in the door. It was a familiar song: the second tests were in and wouldn't you know it? I *had* been chewing spinach in my sleep. Just before I started to fast the night before the test, I had consumed a large spinach salad for dinner. Perhaps it's recovered memory—my mind sitting me on the sofa and taking me through Polaroids of me washing the spinach, now chopping up the leaves, now with a fork headed in the direction of my face—aww, and look at you chewing in this one! You remember, don't you? I now have a vivid recollection of said salad that had escaped me at the time of my original blood test. Not having hemochromatosis and therefore not being concerned about nonspecific stomach pain, I ate enough spinach to throw off the test.

"I can't believe that's possible," I said to the hematologist.

"These things can be tricky." He shrugged. "The human body is a funny thing."

"Hysterical."

I knew I had to make contact with concerned family members but treated myself to a long walk home and a few minutes alone in my apartment first. I lay on the middle of the floor with my knees up, looking at my ceiling. I was not subtly, not perversely, but openly disappointed. I had fallen in love with my flaws once they were easily contained. Every lie I had ever told, every disappointment I had wrought, every botched attempt at normalcy, every successful proof of my inadequacy—all looked practically charming when they shared a raison d'être. I wanted to hold them close but controlled like a balloon tied to my wrist with an IV for a string. If anything went wrong, all I had to do was tug at the string and bring my explanation down for others to see. This is who I am and this is why.

But now my problems had been set loose. They could be any-where at anytime and I was just like everyone else I knew: almost positive that there was something profoundly and undiagnosably wrong with me. I sat up and leaned back on my hands. With my weight on one arm, I lifted the other to my face and wiggled my fingers. I saw nothing, just a hand. I was all grown up, too old to play sick, and robbed of my green ribbon. I looked at the phone. I had calls to make. Important calls to concerned family and friends that would put everything back the way it was, releasing me into the bloodstream of humanity where I would be account-able for my behavior and expected to overcome basic obstacles just like everyone else. I picked up the phone and ordered in sushi.

ACKNOWLEDGMENTS

I am grateful to the many people who made this book what it is—some unwittingly and some on purpose. For the former, I know it's not customary for thieves to leave thank-you notes but: Sorry I broke into your lives. I wouldn't have done it if they weren't so shiny.

For help of the intentional variety, I would like to thank Denise Shannon, whose guidance and sanity has been invaluable. Thank you also to everyone at Riverhead Books for your freakishly instant warmth and brilliance: Sean McDonald, Larissa Dooley, Geoff Kloske, Ben Gibson, Craig Burke and the publicity department. Actually, thank you to pretty much any book publicist ever: there is a streak of the saintly in all of you.

At Knopf, I would like to thank everyone for their generous support and friendship over the years, especially those at Vintage Books. Russell Perreault, Lisa Weinert, Jennifer Jackson and Marty Asher have been amazing colleagues and wonderful friends. A debt of gratitude is also owed to anyone who has ever edited me closer to funny, specifically Suzy Hansen and Ed Park who first said, "You should turn this into an essay," followed by, "Let's get some oatmeal." Josh Kendall and Elizabeth Spiers were early readers and are two of the best people in New York—I am lucky to know them both.

Finally, thank you to the Crosleys. To my mother, who once peeled my eleven-year-old body from the pavement after a horrific bike accident; to my father, who ran no less than three stoplights on the way to the hospital; and to my sister who—as I lay bleeding on a gurney—announced that I had forgotten to put underwear on that morning: I love you more than words can say.